From Skinner to Rogers

THE PROFESSIONAL EDUCATION SERIES

Walter K. Beggs, *Editor*
Dean Emeritus, Teachers College, and
Professor of Educational Administration
University of Nebraska

Royce H. Knapp, *Research Editor*
Regents Professor of Education
University of Nebraska

From Skinner to Rogers

Contrasting Approaches to Education

by

FRANK MILHOLLAN

Associate Professor, Institute for Child Study
University of Maryland

and

BILL E. FORISHA

Instructor of Child and Family Relations
College of Education
Bowling Green State University

PROFESSIONAL EDUCATORS PUBLICATIONS, INC.
LINCOLN, NEBRASKA

Library of Congress Catalog Card No.: 72-88029

ISBN 0-88224-035-8

Contents

Preface

Most teacher education programs provide in one way or another some treatment of the topic of learning and learning theory. When they do not there is an uncomfortable feeling on the part of some students and members of the faculty that an important aspect of teacher education has been neglected. On the other hand, teachers have just as often questioned the value of theories of learning, being, it would appear, more concerned with practical information than with the theoretical speculations of psychologists.

Perhaps a reassessment of our approach to the study of learning and learning theory in education is in order. Several reasons may be suggested for this need, some of which are mentioned below.

Although learning theories are largely a product of this century, even in psychology the study of them has to a great extent become a historical enterprise. New research on learning stimulated by theories has actually declined since the 1950s. There is much greater emphasis now on data collection in the absence of explicit theoretical issues. Also, there is an interest in smaller theoretical problems and in building what are called "miniature systems" which focus on specific problems as opposed to the grandiose theories of learning and behavior of earlier years.

For many years Professor Ernest R. Hilgard in three editions of his book *Theories of Learning* has presented a selection of theories and a rationale for their inclusion.[1] Other authors have been inclined to follow this classification and selection of learning theories. Admittedly, the scientific study of learning has been primarily the domain of psychologists. But educators who have for decades looked to the psychologist for an understanding of the learning process have not often found solutions to their problems. Perhaps the difficulty of applying learning theory to educational practices is due, at least in part, to the *kind* of learning theories upon which we have focused our attention. Many do not deal with the kind of learning that goes on in the classroom. In fact, some contemporary theorists have denied any interest in the practical utility of their findings. Whereas Hilgard's compendium may be highly suited to the needs of psychologists, it is possible that other criteria for selection might better meet the needs of educators.

Perhaps the cry of irrelevancy by educators also arises out of the way in which we have traditionally approached learning theory. It is not unusual to find a few short paragraphs in educational psychology texts devoted to learning theory. What such brief treatment is intended to convey is often obscure. Furthermore, these and even more comprehensive treatments are implicitly or explicitly biased in many instances. Most often theories of learning are presented without adequate development of historical, philosophical, psychological, and educational correlates, which may rob them of potential enrichment of understanding and meaning. In spite of the uncertainty or confusion among students and educators as to the significance of learning theory in teacher preparation, one statement may be agreed upon: *Teaching is an activity which emerges from some conception about how learning occurs.* If this view is accepted, then it is likely that every teacher has some theory of learning which may or may not be readily articulated. It would seem that our task becomes one of identifying ways in which students and teachers may be helped to examine and reflect upon the assumptions and issues which constitute a kind of learning theory appropriate in school settings. If we value the achievement of a synthesis of a teacher's values and goals with his conception of learning and with his educational practice, this goal may be vastly facilitated by a more integrative orientation to the study of learning theory.

The approach of this book has grown both out of classroom teaching experience and out of several years experience in the teaching of learning theories to educators. It is not, however, a survey of learning theories. Rather its primary purpose is to introduce a framework which may serve the reader as a broad basis for evaluation of learning theory, educational philosophy, and educational practice. It is hoped that he may gain a useful and important perspective that would not necessarily be derived from a study of learning theory in itself.

The authors began with the premise that two rather strongly divergent philosophical and psychological viewpoints are represented in current educational literature, much of which is enjoying popular consumption. One or the other of the two viewpoints appears to be reflected to a considerable extent in current educational practice and in proposed reforms and innovations in the schools. And, in fact, almost all modern psychological theories themselves appear to be oriented toward one of these two polar conceptions, which date back to antiquity. These broadly contrasting approaches to the study of man were described by Allport as the Lockean and Leibnitzian traditions.[2] Wann in his book *Behaviorism and Phenomenology: Contrasting Bases for Modern Psychology* edited presentations and associated discussions which clearly illustrate this cleavage in philosophical psychology.[3] Hitt develops the dichotomy further in his conception of "Two Models of Man."[4]

Although the views are represented in the work of a large number of people both historically and contemporarily, the writings of B. F. Skinner and Carl R. Rogers appear to the authors to meet three criteria in keeping with the purposes of this book: They are representative of the two divergent views mentioned above, they are both eminent psychologists who have been interested in and have directed their attention to learning and education, and they both have had and are having considerable influence on educational practice.

It may be interesting to note that, although his system is invariably included in any treatment of learning theory, Skinner disclaims that it is a theory. Rogers, on the other hand, has devoted most of his professional life to the areas of counseling and personality and not, ostensibly, to "learning." As we shall see, both have a great deal to say about learning, although by certain criteria neither are learning theorists.

The primary thrust of the book, then, is the presentation of two divergent models of man, the explicit and implicit philosophical assumptions which characterize each view, the conditions of learning compatible with each model, and the educational implications of each position.

Readers are encouraged to evaluate their own position with regard to the contrasting views presented. It is hoped that this process will provide a sense of direction for teachers, a framework with which to organize educational principles and practices, and guidelines which will assist the student to find his way in the current literature on learning.

Several additional sources for further study are given in the annotated bibliography. They have been selected on the basis of readability, clarity, and solidarity.

PART I

INTRODUCTION

CHAPTER 1

Two Models of Man

Two models or images of man have been proposed and discussed for many years by philosophers and psychologists alike. A symposium held at Rice University in 1964 clearly pointed up the cleavage in contemporary theoretical and philosophical psychology. The main topic of the symposium was the conflict between phenomenology and behaviorism. Addresses and papers presented to the symposium concerned themselves specifically with two distinct models of man and the particular scientific orientation associated with each model. The following statements will describe what appears to be central in this continuing conflict.

The behaviorist orientation considers man to be a passive organism governed by stimuli supplied by the external environment. Man can be manipulated, that is, his behavior controlled, through proper control of environmental stimuli. Furthermore, the laws that govern man are primarily the same as the universal laws that govern all natural phenomena. Therefore, the scientific method, as evolved by the physical sciences, is appropriate as well for the study of the human organism.

The phenomenological orientation considers man to be the source of all acts. Man is essentially free to make choices in each situation. The focal point of this freedom is human consciousness. Behavior is, thus, only the observable expression and consequence of an essentially private, internal world of being. Therefore, only a science of man which begins with experience, as it is immediately given in this world of being, can ever be adequate for a study of the human organism.

Psychologists actually have for several years been concerned with both aspects of man, his actions and his self-awareness. Perhaps, of course, it is not really helpful for an understanding of man to consider these two models or orientations as being, in fact, mutually exclusive. Why must we necessarily choose once and for all between

13

them? Perhaps man can often be described meaningfully in terms of his behavior and at other times or in other contexts can be described more meaningfully in terms of his consciousness (self-awareness). Behavior may indeed be more accessible to traditionally scientific investigations, but a systematic investigation of consciousness might well yield a more significant understanding of man.

Thus, it appears reasonable that man might be described in terms of either his behavior or his self-awareness or both. Nonetheless, in doing so, conclusions about man will remain seemingly contradictory or, at least, paradoxical. They will unavoidably reflect one of the two methodological orientations. And actually, the two models of man would still continue to embody a number of contrasting points of view. Consider these views in the form of the interrelated questions below.

For instance, is man predictable or is he essentially unpredictable? Prediction and control are often considered the final test of validity for any particular scientific theory being advanced. The theory itself is actually an explanation of those sufficient, determining causes of the phenomenon under study. Determinism, which by definition denies human freedom, is thus unavoidably associated with the traditional scientific objective of prediction. But there continues to be notable failures in attempting to predict human behavior; at least one crucial question that arises is whether or not the sufficient causes for behavior can ever really be known, either to the observer or to the subject himself.

Thus the question regarding the possibility of prediction is itself contingent on other questions. Does man live in an objective world? And is he in this world simply a transmitter of information? Or does man live in a subjective world in which he becomes an actual generator of something new? The objective world, it may be put forth, is a reliable, completely rational, measurable entity. Facts and data can be agreed upon to be what they are and to signify additional verifiable information. Man acts in this world as simply an additional element, that is, a live element which has the capacity to transmit information, but not to alter it. An individual exists as a complex machine. In fact, intelligence as such is only that which is fed into the human system. Thus by objective standards human intelligence can be measured and controlled and behavior reflecting this input predicted.

But apparently man also lives in a subjective world. This is a private world of feelings, emotions, and perceptions. From a basis in this private world man does have the capacity to transmit but he has also the higher capacity to generate information anew. He may ask questions that were never before asked. He may make decisions for courses of action that had never before even been contemplated or anticipated. He may even define something as valuable which does not allow for his ability to do so — such as the information-transmitter model of man, which is, of course, acceptable to most behavioral scientists. Man's actions may be guided by scientific knowledge, but they may also be seen to be ultimately determined by an internal experience of choice and valuation. Jaspers (1967) wrote: "An empirical science cannot teach anyone what he ought to do, but only what he can do to reach his end by stable means."[1]

Within this subjective world the individual exists uniquely. That is, from a phenomenological viewpoint each man is unique. In the behavioral sciences laws are developed which are designed to account for whole classes of social phenomena. One man's behavior is predictable precisely because it conforms to such laws. From this objective point of view one man is like other men. Descriptions of man or explanations of his behavior may be most meaningfully represented in absolute terms, that is, in terms free from restriction or limitation. But contrariwise, if each man is considered to be unique, then descriptions or explanation of his behavior must be represented in relative terms. That is, general laws of behavior would not be possible, for everything would be contingent upon something else. In fact, from this viewpoint the very uniqueness of each man's existence precludes any certainty about anything at all.

Related to these questions regarding man's existence in the world as either object or subject is the question: Can man be better understood through analysis or synthesis? Can human characteristics be investigated independently of one another, or must they be studied as a whole? In the behavioral sciences as well as the natural sciences useful results have often been produced by investigating a single characteristic independently of other characteristics. On the other hand, does not such an approach entail the danger of ignoring the importance of the interactions and interdependencies of the many variables operating in any given situation? Perhaps, the most effective strategy would be for the investigator to move back and forth from analysis to synthesis.

In all of these questions we are essentially asking whether or not man is truly knowable in scientific terms or whether or not he is actually more than he can ever know about himself. This final question is basic to the entire study of man. If man exists as a knowable fact, then he constitutes an objective reality. If not, then he exists as a potentiality, that is, he represents possibility rather than actuality.

Maslow (1961) expressed the point of view of human potentiality:
ˣ"I think it fair to say that no theory of psychology will ever be complete that does not centrally incorporate the concept that man has his
future within him, dynamically active at this present moment."[2] Yet,
there is much evidence to support the idea that man is scientifically
knowable. And this evidence is increasing rapidly as a result of both
laboratory experiments and field studies. ˣPerhaps, then it can only
be concluded, however paradoxically, that though man is scientifically
knowable, he is also unknowable in that he probably changes and
evolves each time that he gains new knowledge about himself.

ˣThere are then two possible and traditionally opposed models of
man. The acceptance of either the phenomenological model or the
behaviorist model to the exclusion of the other may have important
implications in the everyday worlds of our personal and professional
lives. This is not just an ongoing debate for the sake of promoting academic exercise. The choice of one or the other could greatly influence
a number of human activities in such areas as education, politics,
theology, parenthood.

This is not to say, however, that a choice must necessarily and
finally be made.ˣ In fact, there appears to be truth in both views of
man. But it is seemingly important that an individual concerned with
working with people be at least familiar with these views and sensi-
tive to the paradoxes involved. It is the purpose of this book to facilitate these processes in the following chapters. ˣThe historical
development of these two models of man will be traced and their contemporary status looked at in some detail.

CHAPTER 2

The Developing Viewpoints

Man has probably always been curious about himself. We can surmise that primitive man's dependence upon his environment would not have permitted him to be indifferent to the effects of his surrounding world upon him. Very early in the history of mankind the living things which shared his world, especially other humans, must have aroused in him a special interest. He must have speculated on their behavior and how he was alike or different from them. It is easy to imagine his asking the familiar questions "What am I?" "How did I come to be what I am?"

We suspect that somehow he stumbled upon the notion of attributing spirits to things that moved as an explanation for their motion. This *animistic* belief system was applied to fire, water, clouds, plants, or to anything which moved. The conclusion that the leaf falls from the tree because the spirit of the leaf or the tree caused it to move may lead us to smile, but animism was important as a first step man took toward understanding nature.

Similar explanations are provided by young children. When the child sees that the trees move when the wind blows, he may come to believe that trees make the wind blow; thus, he is attributing volition to the trees. Although his premise, and consequently his conclusions, are inaccurate, he is seeking causality, which too is an important first step.

It is not implausible to infer that early man eventually accepted the anthropomorphic viewpoint that his behavior as well as that of all animals was accounted for in terms of purposive inner agents or spirits. From the immobility after death, for example, it was assumed that the spirit had left. This spirit which lacks physical dimensions came to be known as the soul, or "psyche" in Greek, the word from which psychology derives its name.

In time every aspect of behavior was attributed to a corresponding feature of the mind or inner person. To some the inner man was

17

seen as driving the body, much as a person drives a car, and speculation on the nature of this inner person or personality was given considerable attention. Furthermore, how the "mind" or inner man related to the physical body and its actions became an important point of departure for those seeking answers to man's nature. The first conjectures about this relationship were recorded by philosophers, eventually becoming known as the "mind-body problem."

Gradually in the course of inquiring into the nature of the universe by ancient philosophers, there arose the question "How *can* we know?" In other words, how can we be sure any knowledge is valid? Later this concern for validity led to inquiries into the question "How *do* we know?" — the processes of knowledge. Very early philosophers had distinguished between knowledge gained by the senses and knowledge achieved by reason. They had noted, too, that knowledge is *human* knowledge and therefore influenced by human ways of knowing. The question which arises next is whether any human mode of conceiving the world can have objective validity; whether inquiring into the ultimate nature of reality is not, after all, quite futile.

Socrates considered the effort futile. But he believed that one kind of knowledge is obtainable — knowledge of the self. This kind of knowledge is needed because it will reveal man's duty and enable him to lead a virtuous life. Socrates believed that virtue is the outcome of knowledge and that evil is fundamentally ignorance. This is an early instance of the belief that the intellectual or rational is dominant in man and morally superior.

Socrates' distinguished pupil Plato was the first to formulate the clear-cut distinction between mind and matter. Plato saw ideas as revealed by reason and things as revealed by the senses. But he saw ideas as far more real than the world known to the senses. Ideas, he noted, have a perfection never present in concrete things. It seemed evident to him that the permanent, perfect, changeless, and absolute in the realm of ideation must be more real than the perishable, changeful, and imperfect objects. He posited, therefore, a world of ideas and a "real" world revealed by the senses which is an imperfect copy of the former. Plato not only distinguished mind and matter, but also associated the terms with opposed sets of values. Mind is good and beautiful; matter is the baser part of man and the universe — a view which has persisted to the present time.

Aristotle, Plato's pupil and successor, found no sharp distinction between mind and matter, or form and matter, as he put it. It seemed to him neither existed apart from the other. Concrete reality arranges itself in a series in which it is impossible to indicate a point on one side of which is matter and on the other form (mind).

In the world of nature Aristotle found matter and form to be related. The body exists for the sake of the soul, but the soul exists only in and through the body. In other words, the activities of the soul are activities of bodily organs. He, then, regarded particular psychological processes as functions of physical structures.

Over the centuries philosophers debated at length many questions about the nature of man which are of concern to us. What is the origin of knowledge or the contents of the mind? What are the differences between man and other animals? Does man have the freedom of choice or are all of his behaviors determined by factors over which he has no control?

In seeking answers to these questions, many philosophers, and eventually psychologists, became aligned with one of two dominant positions regarding the nature of man. These two positions are today represented in the viewpoints we have outlined in the previous chapter—behaviorism and phenomenology. In tracing the modern development of these two views, the line of critical inquiry is usually seen to begin with René Descartes (1596-1650), a philosopher, mathematician, and physiologist. In the aftermath of the Renaissance when the physical and biological sciences were steadily advancing, Descartes saw the need to resolve the conflict between science and religious dogma. Though this was an ambition he never completely fulfilled, he developed views about the nature of man that were to have far-reaching effects.

To the working of the body, he was anxious to apply the principles of physics and held that body is a machine which operates in a determined, lawful fashion. Although it was not until later that the word "reflex" was given to these movements, to Descartes the activities of muscles and tendons, the process of respiration, and even sensation could be explained according to mechanical principles. Since theology accepted that animals have no souls and thus are by definition automata, this statement must also be true of the human body when it is considered without its soul. Descartes saw man, then, as composed of two substances: a reasonable soul, or a thinking substance, which had the power to direct the mechanical course of events, and the body itself. The action of the body, though subject to the direction of the soul, was seen as strictly mechanical. The relation between mind and body was one of interaction—body affects mind and mind affects body. Notwithstanding official church condemnation to the contrary, this position tended to satisfy the theological necessity of the times in keeping the immortal soul distinct from the mortal body.

Thus Descartes resolved the possible incompatibility of a free soul and a mechanically operated body by his *dualism*. This attempt to answer the philosophical questions posed earlier has significance to us because it introduces notions that persist to the present about the nature of man and the acquisition of knowledge. Certain conceptions stemming from this dualism need to be highlighted.

Descartes distinguished man from animals primarily in terms of man's possessing a free soul, a mind capable of choice. Physically man is not unlike animals, whose behaviors are determined mechanically according to physical principles. This is a statement of freedom versus determinism that has remained a philosophical issue to the present.

Scientific pscyhology, as it later became defined by the behaviorists, would not have been established had Descartes' position been permanently accepted. Free agents do not behave according to scientific laws. If the mind were free, they contend, we could not study it or the mechanistic processes of the body, which would be under the capricious control of the mind. Ultimately, any psychologist must reconcile his position on this issue, for if behavior is caused, the task of the psychologist becomes one of seeking the factors internal or external to the organism which can serve to explain behavior. On the other hand, if behavior is capricious, or not attributable to causal factors, the notion of a science of psychology, as traditionally defined, becomes untenable.

It is also important to note that Descartes believed in the existence of innate ideas, ideas not derived from experience. Certain truths (such as conception of God, self, space, time, motion) which formed the basis of all knowledge were inherent in man's nature. It is within this context that the freedom-determinism issue actually evolved. His assertion of innate ideas became the point of departure for a long-standing debate ultimately known as the nature-nurture or heredity-environment issue. This controversy may be subsumed under two systems of thought: *nativism* and *empiricism*.

Nativism, in modern terminology refers to heredity, a person's genetic composition transmitted from his parents. Contemporary efforts have been directed at determining the extent to which human characteristics can be attributed to the gene pool. Nativistic philosophers subscribed to the view that the mental dispositions of man can be attributed to native endowment. Thus it was argued that man is basically morally good or evil, rational or animalistic, active or passive in his relationship to his environment. Nativism, in the extreme, is really an instinct psychology which minimizes the role of the environment in determining man's behavior. The basic properties of man, his intelligence, personality, motives, perceptions, emotions are not conceived as undergoing qualitative change over the life span, but are presumed to exist preformed at birth.

Empiricism, on the other hand, was the philosophical position which sees the characteristics of man as the consequence of experience. The basic assumption of the empirical approach is that intellectual functions can be markedly influenced by the events in a person's life. Today we refer to this position as environmentalism.

Although Descartes had not questioned the existence of innate ideas, the question was raised by some of his critics. In fact, this concern attained such importance that it became the starting point for the long line of inquiry known as British empiricism.

One of the first of these critics was Thomas Hobbes, an older contemporary of Descartes. He reflected the current mode of thought in his notion of the "rational man," the notion that human conduct is dominated by reason. The course of man's actions was seen as planned and foreseen, rather than determined by chance—as directed finally by intellectual considerations as opposed to nonrational feelings, emotions, and accidental events in life. Of more central concern to our discussion, however, is that Hobbes did attempt to account for human activity in a naturalistic way. Sequences of thought, however accidental they may seem, are matters of natural law. Just as ideas are determined by objects acting on the senses, the transitions from one idea to another are determined by the relations they have to each other in the original experience. This is, of course, an expression of a basic principle of associationism: that one idea follows another not by chance but according to law. Hobbes's psychology was entirely mechanistic, materialistic, and deterministic.

It was not Hobbes, however, but his successor, the English philosopher John Locke (1632-1704), who raised the question "How do we know?" that gave the impetus to British empiricism. It was Descartes' doctrine of innate ideas to which Locke principally objected. In answer to the question, how do we gain knowledge about the world or how do we come to know, Locke's answer was that all knowledge comes to us through our senses. Ideas were not inborn; they came from experience. Locke described man's intellect as being a *tabula rasa*, a blank tablet at birth on which sensory experience made its marks. He was, however, only referring to the absence of ideas at birth and not to the complete absence of all predispositions.

Undoubtedly Locke had been influenced by the work of Newton, who had depicted the universe as composed of particles of matter existing in space and time and impelled by force into motion. Locke attempted to explain mind similarly through the combination and interaction of its elements. All mental life was explained through the reduction of the complex to the simple.

For Locke, *ideas* are units of mind, the objects of thinking. Since mind itself is separated from the world of objects, objects which are perceived are only ideas of objects. Ideas are such things as are expressed by the words whiteness, motion, man, elephant. Today we speak of them as concepts or items of knowledge. Since ideas are elements, mind is capable of analysis into ideas. The compounding of complex ideas out of simple ideas is one of the operations of mind. Locke spoke mostly of connections or combinations of ideas, but because he occasionally used the word association, this came to be known as Locke's doctrine of association.

The germ of associationism can be found as far back as Aristotle. He observed that one thing reminds you of another. If A reminds you of B, what is the relation of A to B? His answer was that the relation was sometimes one of *similarity* between the two, sometimes one of *contrast*, and sometimes one of *contiguity* (nearness in time or space). Later these relations were called the laws of association.

For Locke the combinations in which sensations and images occur together in our mind are governed by the laws of association. For example, if the sensation red occurs frequently together with that of heat, eventually a red sensation will bring to mind an idea of heat and vice versa. By this reasoning only material objects affect our senses and all ideas must derive from these. (Such a view is referred to as materialism or materialistic philosophy.)

Our knowledge of the world of things and people to the empiricist, then, was presumed to be built up from sensations piece by piece.

There followed after Locke a long line of philosophers who carried on and developed the associationistic tradition. Whatever the modification introduced along the way, the main line of development was an attempt to show that starting with elements (ideas) and the general principle of association, it is possible to account for all mental functions, no matter how complex. We shall come back to the associationists a little later.

Perhaps the most extreme of the nativist positions was represented by Gottfried Leibnitz (1646-1716), a contemporary of John Locke, whose views he opposed. In Leibnitz' system the element of all being, simple or complex, physical or mental, was the *monad*. Monads were considered dynamic, continuously active and developing according to their own laws. They are not susceptible to external influence and have no effect on one another; consequently there are no causes. A monad is like a watch perfectly constructed, indestructible, wound up and set going forever. It continues without external agents, according to laws of its own nature. Two such watches always agree and yet neither is the cause of the other. Cause as anything more than coincidence is illusory. Harmony exists in nature because harmony exists in the laws of monads.

Since man's body and mind represent different but parallel aspects of the same basic substance, they too operate according to their own inner laws. Mind is a continuously active entity not impelled by chance external events, but rather pulled by the long-term goal of its own ultimate perfection. The human being may come into the world, not with ideas fully formed, but with tendencies and predispositions that make the development of certain ideas highly probable. The inner determinants of behavior in Leibnitz' system are stressed.

In his book *Becoming,* Gordon Allport interprets the position of Leibnitz in this way:

> To Leibnitz the intellect was perpetually active in its own right, addicted to rational problem solving, and bent on manipulating sensory data according to its own inherent nature. For Locke the organism was reactive when stimulated; for Leibnitz it was self-propelled. . . . The Leibnitzian tradition . . . maintains that the person is not a collection of acts, nor simply the locus of acts; the person is the source of acts. And activity itself is not conceived as agitation resulting from pushes by internal or external stimulation. It is purposive. To understand what a person is, it is necessary always to refer to what he may be in the future, for every state of the person is pointed in the direction of future possibilities.[1]

We see, then, in the philosophies of Locke and Leibnitz the rather clear formulation of certain questions about man's nature and their contrasting answers that are representative of the behavioristic and phenomenological traditions which followed. Although all issues in psychology cannot be neatly ordered in terms of this basic dichotomy, as Allport has suggested, "virtually all modern psychological theories appear oriented toward one of two polar conceptions."[2]

Is man governed from within or governed from without? Is man active and initiating or merely reactive to external stimulation? Is there a free will, freedom of choice and self-determination, or are man's actions determined "mechanically" largely by causal influence in our environment?

The tradition that began with Locke developed from the premise that knowledge comes from external stimulation, that man is a "receiver and transmitter" of information. Acceptable to this view is the notion of causality, of determinism—that events can be explained in terms of their antecedents. For Leibnitz knowledge is derived from within; man is a "generator" of information. Mind is active and free of causality; causal efficacy in behavior is attributed to the volition of the person.

Allport points out that perhaps it was because Locke was an Englishman that his way of thinking became so firmly established in Britain and America, whereas Leibnitz' view, developed later by Kant in Germany, has generally prevailed on the Continent.[3] Certainly in the United States there has been a predominantly environmentalistic orientation in psychology. There have always been vigorous opponents to any suggestion that our genes could have any determining effect upon intelligence, personality, or other psychological characteristics. Undoubtedly our dominant political and social attitudes were important in shaping the environmentalist position. Since all men are created equal, education and socioeconomic reform are the answers to self-fulfillment. Such goals are particularly meaningful if man is perceived as being almost infinitely modifiable. This viewpoint favored the study of learning as a problem area in psychology and the development of learning theory, essentially an American phenomenon.

Since for Locke knowledge was a product of interaction with the environment, his thinking opened the way for psychologists and educators to place emphasis upon environmental nurture rather than hereditary nature. In school this meant, even in Locke's day, teachers were to build minds of children by a systematic instructional program.

From the standpoint of psychology Locke is at the starting-point of two movements. One line of critical inquiry was the attack on the rational view of man in psychology. This was a system of thought which, claiming a knowledge of the soul that was based on intuitions and deductions, held that its knowledge was demonstrable as absolutely valid. The other was a more positive movement which led to a psychology that was empirical as opposed to rational, but which fell short of becoming experimental. This is known as British empiricism, the philosophical view that experience is the only source of knowledge.

Following Locke, the English philosopher George Berkeley (1685-1753) believed that all knowledge is derived from sensation and no other source. Solidity and all other primary qualities are known only through perception. An apple, for example, is *all* sensation and is *nothing but* sensation. Consequently there is no material substance; we know only sensory qualities.

David Hume (1711-76) questioned both the existence of the thinking self and the principle of causality. When trying to examine the self, he found nothing but specific perceptions like love or hate, pleasure or pain, light or shade but nothing that corresponded to self. Similarly, he disposed of the notion of causality. When he traced an idea back to the experiences from which it presumably was derived, he found no necessary connection or causality. He found only contiguity and succession. All we see is A followed by B. Causality is nowhere to be found in experience; it is only a product of the mind and has no objective validity.

British associationism was derived from the mode of thought that characterized Locke and his successors. Associationism asserted that learning and the development of higher processes consist mainly in the combination of supposedly irreducible mental elements. Hobbes, Locke, Berkeley, and Hume all contributed, but Daniel Hartley (1705-57) formulated the basic doctrine. According to Hartley, there are two orders of events to be taken into account, the mental and the physical. These two orders are not identical, but run parallel to each other; a change in one is thus accompanied by a change in the other. Sensations and ideas are directly connected. The general law of association is that if sensations have often been experienced together, the corresponding ideas will tend to occur together. If A has been associated with B, C, and D in sensory experience, the sensory experience A, occurring alone, will tend to rouse the idea of B, C, and D.

Many other philosophers followed in this tradition but space prevents our discussion of them all. Whatever modifications were introduced by other associationists, the main purpose was an attempt to show that starting with ideas and the general principle of association, it was possible to account for all mental functions, no matter how complex. The main concern of these men was the attempt to discover natural laws in a world of observable, natural events.

Following Leibnitz, mentioned earlier as representing the nativist view, there is a rather clear line of succession in Germany.

The German philosopher Christian Wolff (1679-1754) represented two habits of thought that had to be eradicated in order for psychology to become "scientific." One was that rational psychology has direct access to truth and reality in a way accessible to natural science, that truth about the soul is attainable by the exercise of pure reason. The other was the conception that the soul or mind is endowed innately with powers or faculties which explain the specific performances of the mind. This faculty psychology met its most effective adversary in the psychology of Johann Friedrich Herbart, which displaced it. Wolff put forth the view that mind has distinct faculties. The basic factors are knowing, feeling, and willing, and the knowing faculty is divided into several others, including perception, imagination, memory, and pure reason. Faculties are present at birth, and education is the training of these faculties through repeated exercise. For example, will is an ability to implement effectively a decision which has been made. It is strengthened by hard work, doing unpleasant tasks, or doing things one does not want to do. The use of force and severe punishment was appropriate to strengthen the will and thus inhibit evil tendencies.

Immanuel Kant (1724-1804), in his remarkably influential book, *Critique of Pure Reason,* insisted that the world as we know it is a world of order, but this order cannot be derived from experience. It must come from the mind itself, which, instead of reflecting the order in our external world, imposes its own laws upon nature. Experience, according to Kant, is a product of things as they are in themselves and of the mind. Experience begins when things act upon the senses, but when this happens an elaborate machinery is set going that makes it impossible for us to know things as they are. Things in themselves can never be known; they can only be known as they appear in experience, influenced by our thoughts. Nature can never be discovered; reality, as it exists outside our experience, is forever beyond our reach. It is as impossible to know the soul as it is the world. Therefore, rational psychology, claiming to have direct knowledge of the soul, is impossible.

The effect of Kant upon psychology was to reaffirm subjectivism and the importance of mental phenomena which cannot be reduced to body processes. After Kant it was natural for the developing experimental psychology in Germany to become a science of consciousness. In England, Russia, and America it was easier for psychology to become objective than in Germany, which remained true to consciousness, to phenomenal experience.

Johann Friedrich Herbart (1776-1841) is best known as the father of scientific pedagogy, which is based upon psychology. Besides being an educational theorist, however, he also occupies an important place in the history of psychology. Herbart's philosophy is derived primarily from Leibnitz. He believed psychology to be an empirical science but not experimental. Observation, not experiment, is the method of psychology.

It may be interesting to note at this point that the term "empirical" has to do with experience, but the word has two meanings in German, which were commonly confused in translation. One refers to present experience, that which is immediately there for the observer without reference to its origin. The other refers to the accumulation of past experience. For the phenomenologist empirical data is present experience, primarily, though he accepts past experience. For the behaviorist the acquisition and accumulation of experiences is the focus. Thus both positions are empirically based and from Herbart's stand, both are scientific.

Like the British associationists Herbart undertook to explain the most complex mental phenomena in terms of simple ideas. He emphasized the idea of inhibition as well as of association. Every idea has the tendency to maintain itself and to drive out ideas with which it is incompatible; and ideas vary in strength. When an idea encounters a stronger idea or group of ideas with which it is incompatible, it is driven below the level of consciousness. The idea is not destroyed, however, but persists, though for the time it is unconscious. An idea that is in itself weak may gain admittance to consciousness, and maintain itself there, if the ideas above the threshold are congenial with it. Ideas already in possession of the field regularly repel uncongenial ideas; but uninhibited ideas, following the tendency of all ideas to rise to consciousness, are assimilated to the ideas in consciousness at the time. This process Herbart called *apperception*, and the group of ideas into which the entering idea is introduced is known as the *apperceptive mass*. For a time, teachers everywhere were made acquainted with the five steps of the Herbartian technique, a method designed to build up in the pupil's mind an apperceptive mass suitable to the reception of new material to be presented.[4]

Herbart's belief in a scientific psychology founded upon experience is a view which has persisted to the present. His metaphysical foundation for psychology, however, has not survived. Herbart's metaphysics led him to substitute *a priori* generalizations for inductions based upon observations. He was unwilling afterward to appeal to experimental verification. Herbart represents, therefore, a transition from the pure speculation of Kant to the experimental psychology of Wundt, whom we consider next.

Although the psychological problems of mind and of knowing had been the domain of philosophers, during the nineteenth century psychology evolved as an independent discipline. British empiricism and associationism had formed the chief philosophical preparation for scientific psychology. There were no "scientific" psychologists until well after 1860. Between 1800 and 1860, however, there were physiologists and physicists who contributed to psychology through their study of the nervous system and sensation. The physical sciences could claim great success for the experimental method. The atomic theory of matter, which stated that all complex substances could be analyzed into component elements, had been supported by experimental evidence. Since these first scientific "psychologists" were indeed physiologists and physicists, it is not surprising that they applied the same principles and methods to the problems of psychology. It was inevitable, perhaps, that knowledge of the physiology of the nervous system would have special significance to psychology. Locke and other empiricists had long before developed the view that knowledge comes to us through our senses. Later the associationists sought the elements of experience — sensation. The sensory physiologists looked for the bodily processes underlying those sensations. They looked for the receptor organ and the specific nerve energies corresponding to every sensation. Since neither of these could be found for shape, size, or distance, they were assumed to be combinations of more basic sensations, built up through past experience, as originally suggested by the empiricist philosophers. The work of sensory physiologist and associationistic philosopher had converged to constitute experimental physiological psychology, the systematic study of mental elements and their combination.

The very strong influence of Wilhelm Wundt (1832-1920) was perhaps a major determining factor in shaping the new psychology. Wundt himself was training in medicine and later turned first to physiology and then to psychology. It is customary to cite the establishment of psychology as a science in 1879, when Wundt founded his psychological laboratory in Leipzig, Germany. However, in 1860 Gustav Fechner (1801-87) published *Elements of Psychophysics*, which is taken by some to mark the beginning of experimental psychology.

Wundt's psychology has been referred to as structuralism, an attempt to study the structure of the mind. He and his colleagues searched for mental elements into which all mental contents could be analyzed. The element, they thought, must be sensation, such as green, sour, cold. To search for these elements and the rules for combining them, they used a method known as *introspection*. Subjects were exposed to a physical stimulus, analyzed their state of awareness, and reported the results of that analysis. They were trained to report as objectively as possible what they experienced and to disregard the meanings they had come to associate with the particular stimulus. It was anticipated that the mental content of an experience would be reconstructed from elementary sensations.

German psychology, after Wundt, became the standard for the rest of Europe and for America as well. Many American psychologists received their training with Wundt. But Wundt's kind of psychology was never completely accepted in America for a variety of reasons. Europeans were not interested in applied psychology, whereas American psychologists were very much concerned with the practical uses of psychology. For them the prevailing kind of psychology was dull, sterile, and going nowhere. Other psychologists objected to the subjective, mentalistic flavor of structuralism and to the methods it utilized. Out of the dissatisfactions emerged many new movements, each of which defined its content and methodology and in most respects amplified philosophical differences. One of these systems, known as behaviorism, follows in the Lockean tradition and will be described in Chapter 3. Another, which will be considered in Chapter 6, is more closely identified with the Leibnitzian tradition and is referred to as Gestalt psychology, or phenomenology.

From this survey of the philosophical background of psychology, we have emphasized the emergence of two contrasting conceptions of man and sources of knowledge. On the one hand, those identified with the Lockean tradition see mind as a blank tablet by nature. It is not genetic predispositions so much as what happens to the organism that determines his behavior and his characteristics. Consequently, what is external is more fundamental than what is not an environmentalist orientation. Furthermore, there is a predisposition to explain complex mental functions through the combination and interaction of elements — to reduce the large or molar to units which are small and molecular. Very largely through the efforts of Wundt, psychology was established by imitating the aims and practices of the natural sciences — although there were predispositions to do so as far back as Locke. Even though the subject matter of the new science was conscious experience and its method introspection, the Lockean tradition was clearly dominant at the end of the nineteenth century.

The Leibnitzian tradition, on the other hand, established the view that knowledge is derived from within — that man generates knowledge. Man is active, free of causality, and the determiner of his own destiny. Nature can never be discovered, for reality, as it exists outside of our experience, is forever beyond our reach. Present experience takes precedence as empirical data over the accumulation and acquisition of experiences. For those identified with this tradition, their objection to psychology's identification with the natural sciences arises principally because they believe that the assumptions of the natural sciences are inappropriate for the study of man.

In the chapters which follow, we will focus our attention on the more contemporary developments within these traditions and their significance to education.

PART II

A SCIENTIFIC PSYCHOLOGY: B. F. SKINNER

In a survey of departmental chairmen of American universities, Harvard's Skinner was chosen overwhelmingly as the most influential figure in modern psychology. It has been conjectured that he will be known as the major contributor to psychology in this century. Without question he is the most controversial contemporary figure in psychology today.

Skinner's contribution consists to a great extent of developing the study of behavior into an objective science. Through experiments with positive and negative reinforcement on laboratory animals, he has learned to predict and control their behavior. His "Skinner box," an apparatus in which the experiments have been carried out, is now standard equipment in most psychological laboratories.

His contributions are not limited to scientific psychology. His fictional account of a Utopian society based on the scientific control of human behavior, *Walden Two*,[1] has sold nearly a half million copies. His latest book, *Beyond Freedom and Dignity*,[2] described as a non-fiction version of *Walden Two*, delivers the message that we can no longer afford freedom, and so it must be replaced with control over man, his conduct, and his culture. This thesis accounts in part for the alarm and anger that Skinner's current popularity arouses in his opponents.

His development of the first device for programed instruction may be leading to what many experts are calling a revolution in American education. Almost all educators today are familiar with the Skinner-inspired teaching machines.

While his contributions to psychology have brought him the respect of scientists throughout the world, they have also brought him the enmity of humanists and psychoanalysts. He is seen by some as the archetype of the cold-blooded scientist for whom man is simply a machine that can be trained to do his bidding.

It is doubtful that any educator has been unaffected by Skinner's work and his views. School practices have been influenced by the principles of operant conditioning; knowingly or unknowingly, teachers have applied these principles in the classroom — most often haphazardly and inconsistently by Skinner's standards. In view of its strong influence today both in psychology and education, a rather thorough description of Skinner's system is provided in the pages which follow.

An understanding of his position, it would seem, may be vastly facilitated by the description of some appropriate antecedents. Although it would be presumptuous to suggest specific influences upon Dr. Skinner, the work of a number of persons preceding him bears sufficient similarities to his efforts to warrant inclusion here: Thorndike and connectionism, Pavlov and classical conditioning, and Watson and behaviorism are briefly described in Chapter 3, along with some of Skinner's views concerning a "science of human behavior." As you shall see, Part II develops the Lockean associationistic, environmentalistic tradition as expressed in the work of more contemporary psychologists.

Chapter 4 describes in some detail Skinner's conception of the learning process and Chapter 5 presents some educational implications of his work.

CHAPTER 3

Historical and Philosophical Background

One of B. F. Skinner's major contributions is his experimental analysis of the consequences of behavior and how they may change the probability that the behavior which produced them will occur again. Many words in the English language, such as "reward" and "punishment," refer to this effect.

Rewards and punishments as regulators of human conduct have a long history. Many of our educational, social, and legal practices are based on the assumption that behavior is modified by rewarding or punishing consequences. It is generally assumed that actions followed by rewards are strengthened, while actions followed by punishment are weakened or extinguished. The experimental investigation of this assumption, however, was first undertaken about 1898 by Edward L. Thorndike (1874-1949).

Thorndike and Connectionism

Thorndike perhaps more than any other person made learning, particularly learning by rewarding consequences, a central concept in psychology. The principles and concepts which he developed from almost 50 years of research were unquestionably a major influence not only on the psychology of learning but upon educational practice in America as well.

Several streams of influence may be identified in the work of Thorndike (as well as that of Pavlov and Watson). Clearly among them are (1) the evolutionary theory of Darwin and studies of animal behavior which followed and (2) the associationistic tradition.

The psychological study of animals arose in part from the interest of physiologists in the sense organs and behavior of various kinds of animals. On the basis of his work on the nervous system, Pierre Flourens proposed that conclusions drawn from animal experimentation should be equally applicable to man. This view gained wide acceptance because it was much more convenient to experiment with animals than with human subjects. But its chief significance, perhaps, lies in the inference that findings of animal studies can be used to explain human behavior.

Perhaps the major impetus, however, came from Darwin and the theory of evolution. If there is continuity between man and all other animals in respect to bodily structure, is it not plausible to assume kinship in respect to mental or emotional attributes? Furthermore, if our physical characteristics have evolved from some early animal ancestor, could not our mental characteristics have developed from a primitive animal mind?

Such conjectures aroused heated opposition by theologians and by the common man, who saw himself as quite different from animals and vastly superior. Whereas animal behavior was regarded as being guided by instinct, man's behavior was considered rational — guided by reason.

Early evolutionists collected examples of animal behavior which appeared to depend upon reasoning, and a vast repertory of such instances was developed. Unfortunately the only alternatives considered to explain animal behavior were either instincts or reasoning. It remained for Thorndike and his contemporaries to include the broader choice between instinct and learning.

Experimental study of animal learning had been suggested earlier, however, by Wundt in Germany and by Lloyd Morgan in England. Both of these men had conducted a few experiments and had rejected the notion of reasoning, at least in dogs. Wundt concluded that dogs learned by forming simple associations and Morgan that it was attributable to trial and error. Since in either case the facts of the animal's behavior could be explained without assuming higher mental processes, both recommended what is known as the *law of parsimony*. Morgan's canon, as it has been called, states that in no case may we interpret an action as the outcome of a higher mental process, if it can be interpreted as the outcome of one which stands lower in the psychological scale.

Anthropomorphic explanations of animal behavior still persist in the nonscientific community. We often devise grandiose explanations for the behavior of our pets. Affection is attributed to the cat when he jumps on our lap, when a more parsimonious explanation may be that warmth is provided by our body and he was cold.

The stage had been set by Wundt and Morgan. The observed facts pointing to evidences of thinking could be explained in other ways, ways in which the assumption of inner thought processes were not required. Thorndike became convinced that animal behavior was little mediated by ideas, by thought processes, and he focused his efforts on an alternative explanation—learning.

The second important influence in Thorndike's work was undoubtedly the associationistic tradition. Thorndike assumed that learning is the formation of associative bonds, or *connections,* the process of linking physical and mental events in various combinations. The physical events were stimuli and responses, and mental events were things sensed or perceived. Learning is the process of selecting and connecting these physical and mental units. But true to the associationistic tradition, this process was a passive, mechanical, or automatic one. Responses were said to be made directly to the situation as sensed. Although Thorndike preferred the terms "selecting and connecting," the terms "trial and error" became popularized and found their way into the vocabularies of educators and psychologists. Thornkike was impressed by the characteristic "trial and error" nature of the behavior of his experimental subjects. He concluded that learning was largely a matter of stamping in correct responses and stamping out incorrect ones as a result of their pleasurable or annoying consequences, i.e., rewards or punishments. He called this stamping in or out by the consequences the Law of Effect. This law was established in his famous research with cats and puzzle boxes.

Thorndike prepared puzzle boxes for cats, boxes in which the animal was confined and from which it could escape by clawing a rope or pushing up a bobbin or even by doing three different things. Usually a cat went through a long process of walking around, clawing the sides of the box, and other responses before it made the appropriate response leading to escape. Thorndike plotted learning curves, showing how long it took the cat to get out on each trial. On successive trials, the cats took less and less time to get out. However, the improvement was gradual. This led Thorndike to conclude that the learning involved a gradual stamping in of the stimulus-response connections between seeing the rope and pulling it. The animals learned by trial and error and accidental success, not by intelligent understanding of the relation between rope-pulling and door-opening. It was plain that the success of the correct movement, although it came after the movement, caused that movement to be learned. Traces of the past were stamped in so that the past might thereafter more readily occur.

Besides the laws of association, which no doubt strongly influenced Thorndike, associationists alluded to trial and error learning, reflexes and instincts as the basis of habits, and the hedonistic principle. The latter was particularly significant in the formulation of the Law of Effect.

Hedonism is the theory that human action arises out of the desire of men to gain pleasure and avoid pain. As a theory of motivation this failed to satisfy the experimental psychologist because of the difficulty in defining what might be pleasurable or painful to a given organism. Furthermore, it is difficult to demonstrate how something in the future has bearing on the behavior of animals. This would be attributing thought processes to animals, thus violating the law of parsimony. By postulating that the consequences of an animal's acts strengthen the acts they follow, one avoids the problem of teleology (seeking explanations of behavior by reference to future situations). A response that has been strengthened through the Law of Effect is more likely to occur in later similar situations. No reference need be made to goals or future events. Purpose must push, not pull. It lies within the organism, not in the future and outside of him.

This problem in motivation remains as one of the distinguishing features between various psychological theories. Must we confine our concept of motives to drives and rewards or reinforcers, an essentially mechanical approach? Or must we include the concept of purpose and goal-seeking, a more complex thought process, and consequently a less parsimonious explanation, in accounting for the motivation of man and other animals?

Although Thorndike's early work was concerned with the nature of animal learning, he later applied the principles derived from animal studies to problems of human learning. He was convinced that the fundamental laws of learning hold true regardless of wide differences among species. If an alternative to reasoning in animals had been found, could not the same principle be applied to human behavior? If thought processes were not needed to explain the behavior of cats, need they be used to explain human action?

A comparison of the learning curves of human subjects with those of animals led him to believe that the same essentially mechanical phenomena disclosed by animal learning are the fundamentals of human learning also. Although always aware of the greater subtlety and range of human learning, he showed a strong preference for understanding more complex learning in terms of the simpler, and for identifying the simpler forms of human learning with that of animals.

When Thorndike began his experimental work on learning, two influential theories had made their mark on educational thinking, both of which Thorndike attacked. One was the developmental theory of G. Stanley Hall (1846-1924). He was an evolutionist and believed that the development of the individual recapitulates the evolution of the race. Education, according to Hall, should be geared to these cycles of racial development. Hall's basic conceptions stressed the importance of heredity, which limited the power of education to change man. At a time when the country was beginning to accept the notion that social progress depended upon education, the notion of inherited determining tendencies was unacceptable. Consequently, Thorndike's learning theory was well received by educational and social theorists. It was supportive of a concept that man was almost infinitely modifiable, an idea that had appeal. Although Thorndike accepted instinctive tendencies in man, as most people of his time did, he tried to make it clear that these tendencies could be supplemented, redirected or even reversed through learning. The capacity to learn is part of the organism's nature.

The other prevailing theory which Thorndike demolished was the formal discipline theory of education. According to this doctrine, education is a process of disciplining or training minds. Mental faculties are strengthened through exercises, very much as we exercise our muscles. Supporters of Latin and Greek or formal mathematics tried to justify teaching them in the schools on the basis of their being the best subject matter for strengthening such faculties as memory or reasoning. Thorndike's experiments attempted to demonstrate the fallacy in formal discipline theory which accepted such general transfer. Transfer of learning occurs when learning in one situation influences learning and performance in other situations. For Thorndike transfer takes place only to the extent that there are identical elements in the two situations. These may be identities of substance or procedure. Ability to speak and write are important in many tasks in life; transfer will be effected through what the different situations require in common. Even if the substance is different, there may be procedures in common. If an activity is learned more easily because another activity was learned first, it is only because the two activities overlap. Learning is always specific, never general. When it appears to be general, it is only because new situations have much of old situations in them.

Schools are publicly supported in the hope that more general uses will be made of what is learned in school. To some extent all schooling is aimed at a kind of transfer beyond the school. Thorndike's theory of transfer led to a very specific and practical curriculum in the schools. Teachers should teach for transfer. The school program should include as many learning tasks as possible which will contribute to effective performance outside of school.

Part of Thorndike's appeal may be attributed to the quantitative nature of his system. Science had established a strong foothold and a psychology of learning that accepted that "anything that exists, exists in an amount and is therefore measurable" was bound to find support. But Thorndike was interested in schools and school problems and in individual differences. He tried to show educators what psychology had to offer. Since learning is connecting, teaching is the arrangement of situations which will lead to appropriate bonds and make them rewarding. The stimulus and response must be distinguished in order that their connection may be achieved.

At the time Thorndike was performing his early experiments and demonstrating what he called the Law of Effect, Pavlov in Russia, working with dogs, established evidence for the comparable principle he called reinforcement. This is an illustration of a simultaneous but independent discovery that has quite often occurred in science.

Pavlov and Classical Conditioning

The doctrine of association had been the basis for explaining memories and how one idea leads to another. Aristotle provided the basic law, association by contiguity. We remember something because in the past we had experienced that something together with something else. Seeing a short gun may remind you of a murder or it may remind you of a hunting experience in Wyoming, depending on your past history. When you hear the word "table" you are likely to think of "chair." "Carrots" makes you think of "peas"; "bread" makes you think "butter"; and so on. In each case the two items had for you been experienced contiguously—in the same place or at the same time or both. Today the terms stimulus and response are used to describe the two units which have been associated by contiguity.

Classical conditioning is an expression of the doctrine of association as based on the laboratory research of the Russian physiologist Ivan P. Pavlov (1849-1936). For Pavlov, the learning process was a matter of the formation of an association between a stimulus and a reflexive response through contiguity. A stimulus is considered an energy change in the environment to which an organism reacts and is usually symbolized as S. The reflex or response is symbolized by R. For Pavlov, learning involved some kind of connection in the central nervous system between an S and an R. Essentially what happens in conditioning is that one stimulus is substituted for another. This is often referred to as a stimulus substitution process. Let us examine the process in closer detail.

All of us are aware that certain stimuli automatically produce or elicit rather specific responses we call *reflexes*. Previous learning seems not to be required for such behavior as sneezing, coughing, dilation and contraction of the pupil of the eye, perspiration. A great many reflexes have been identified in infants shortly after birth. Some disappear and others appear later in life.

We may also have observed that at times the reflex occurs in response to stimuli that appear to be only indirectly related to the response. Perhaps the most common is salivation to the smell of food, such as bacon frying, or the sight of a sizzling steak. Pavlov made extensive use of the salivary reflex in his pioneering studies of this phenomenon. His work profoundly influenced the development of learning theory in the United States.

While studying gastric secretions in dogs, Pavlov devised apparatus to collect and measure saliva secreted by the dogs in response to food placed in their mouths. He noted incidentally that the dogs would begin to salivate before the food actually reached the mouth. The sight of the food dish, the approach of an attendant or even the sound of footsteps each became sufficient to induce salivation. Pavlov recognized that the sight of the food dish and other stimuli had come through experience to be a signal to the dog that food would follow. He decided to systematically study this reaction, which he called a *conditional reflex*. The procedure he used is called classical conditioning today.

The often-cited illustration of this kind of experiment is training the dog to salivate to a tuning fork tone. The dog was securely fastened in the apparatus and the stimuli in the laboratory were carefully controlled. The tuning fork was sounded in the presence of the dog to be sure that it did not salivate to the tone before conditioning. The sound of the tuning fork was presented to the dog and within seconds meat powder was forced through a tube into his mouth producing the normal reflex flow of salvia. This exact procedure was repeated a number of times. After a number of such repetitions saliva began to flow at the sound of the tuning fork without presentation of the meat powder. This was the conditional response. A previously neutral stimulus had acquired the power to elicit a response which was originally elicited by another stimulus. The change occurred when the neutral stimulus was followed or "reinforced" by the effective stimulus, meat powder.

In order to establish the conditional response so that it would be available day to day often required several days of conditioning. Once established, however, it was retained over a long period of disuse. One of Pavlov's important discoveries was the *extinction* of the conditional response. A well-established conditional response could be extinguished by presenting the tone a number of times, without receiving meat powder; the flow of saliva declined with each repetition until it disappeared altogether. If the tone had during conditioning become a signal that food was coming, it had during extinction become a signal that no food was coming. Under conditions of extinction the dog became visibly drowsy as opposed to his previous readiness for action. Such extinction was not regarded by Pavlov as a permanent loss or forgetting, because after an interval of rest the dog would again salivate to the tone. This was called *spontaneous recovery*. Eventually, however, spontaneous recovery in the cycle occurred less and less and finally the response would not recover at all.

Pavlov also found that once a conditional reflex had been established to a given tone, a conditional response would to some extent transfer to one of another pitch. The effective conditioned stimulus seemed to generalize, within limits, to similar stimuli. The less similar the new stimulus to the original one, however, the weaker the conditional response. The principle of generalization is familiar to all of us. We need not be taught specifically to recognize each different model and year of automobiles *as* automobiles; nor do we have difficulty in recognizing a specific grocery store even though we had not seen that one before. Even children understand the principle of generalization as based on prior experience with similar stimuli.

Another important finding of Pavlov was that *stimulus differentiation* (or discrimination) was achieved when he delivered meat powder to one stimulus but not to other similar stimuli. A dog which salivated to a metronome at 100 beats per minute also salivated to 80 and 120 beats per minute, as stimulus generalization would lead us to expect. By presenting meat powder with 100 beats per minute, but not with the 80- or 120-beat stimuli, differentiation occurred. The dog continued to respond to 100 beats per minute, whereas the conditional response to the other stimuli extinguished.

If the differentiation requirements became too fine for the dog, such as trying to establish a distinction between 95 and 100 beats per minute, a condition that Pavlov called *experimental neurosis* was seen to develop. The dog became visibly disturbed and responded at random to either stimulus. The uncontrolled behavior reappeared whenever he returned to the apparatus.

The important features of Pavlovian theory are essentially those which have been described. It is possible that Pavlov's conditioning principles apply principally to emotional responses. If this is true, since all behavior seems to include emotional concomitants to some degree, Pavlovian principles apply to the degree to which we are "emotionally involved." People are, in general, conditioned to respond favorably or unfavorably to anything that can function as a stimulus. It is possible that our interests and preferences, our attitudes, our fears, hates, and loves, and even the connotative meaning of words are acquired through classical conditioning. Considerable controversy still exists, however, and much more research is needed to establish this explanation of affective learning. The interested reader is encouraged to seek further information in this area.

Watson and Behaviorism

In spite of the fact that Wilhelm Wundt years before had been credited with founding "physiological psychology" and had written on the subject of the nervous system, his psychology was largely mentalistic. His influence led to the minimizing of interest in the body in psychology. It was much later that psychologists, principally in America, began to insist that the body be brought back into psychology. These psychologists argued that psychology could become a true science only if it changed its focus from conscious experience to the study of behavior. They believed that psychological experience is private knowledge which cannot be observed and verified by others and, consequently, lies outside the realm of science. The intangible events of consciousness as reported by introspective methods seemed very unscientific, and for psychology to become a recognized science was very important to many psychologists. Scientists generally are interested in evidence that is publicly verifiable: in other words, data which is open to observation by others, which is studied in the same manner by any number of researchers, and which leads to uniform conclusions. The leading spokesman for this kind of psychology which became known as behaviorism was John B. Watson (1878-1958).

Behaviorism as a system of psychology was first announced by Watson in an article entitled *Psychology as the Behavorist Views It*, published in 1913. While teaching at Johns Hopkins University, he became dissatisfied with psychology as the science of conscious experience. His field of research was animal psychology. It had long been recognized that consciousness in animals can neither be directly observed nor logically proved to exist. Yet it was possible to study and learn a great deal about animals simply by observing their behavior. Traditional psychologists considered animal research in learning and problem-solving to be unimportant. Watson, taking the offensive, claimed that non-introspective, non-mentalistic animal research was the only true research. Furthermore, since it was possible to dispense with animal consciousness, he believed the same approach could be used with human beings—by abolishing conscious experience and studying human behavior. Thus it was Watson who made the first clear proposal that psychology should be regarded simply as a science of behavior.

Human behavior was to be studied objectively. Because consciousness was not objective, it was not scientifically valid and could not be studied. By behavior Watson meant the movements of muscles and activities of glands. For him thought, for example, could only be studied as movements of the throat, since thought for him was simply subvocal speech. Feelings and emotions similarly were movements of the viscera. Thus, Watson disposed of all mentalism in favor of a purely objective science of behavior.

Besides rejecting the study of consciousness, he vehemently attacked the analysis of motivation in terms of instincts. At the time Watson's career began it was common to "explain" almost any form of behavior—human as well as animal—as due to a particular instinct. Social behavior was attributed to an instinct of gregariousness, fighting to an instinct of aggressiveness, child care to a maternal instinct, and so on. These were assumed to be innate. Watson objected both to the mentalistic nature of instincts and to the assertion that such behavior was innate. We are not born with social behavior—we learn it. Watson denied that we are born with any particular mental abilities, personality traits, or even predispositions. We inherit only our physical structure and a few reflexes, and all other differences among us are attributed to learning.

Thus Watson took a strong stand for the environmentalist position; human nature for him is greatly subject to change and there is practically no limit to what man might become.

Watson's psychology was certainly in the tradition of the empiristic philosophy of John Locke and was clearly influenced by the physiological psychology of Ivan Pavlov. Upon learning of Pavlov's work, Watson quickly accepted classical conditioning as the explanation for all of learning. We are born with certain stimulus-response connections called reflexes. We build an array of new stimulus-response connections by the process of conditioning. More complex behaviors are learned by building up series of reflexes. In walking, for example, all responses such as putting one foot forward, putting weight on that foot, swinging the other foot forward and so forth are separate reflexes which, occurring in the proper sequence, constitute a skilled performance.

Watson did accept three emotional reaction patterns as innate — fear, anger, and love. They are similar to reflexes and all other emotional reactions are learned in association with them. They refer to patterns of movement, not conscious feelings. Emotional learning involves the conditioning of these three patterns of emotional response to new stimuli. The conditioning of a fear response was demonstrated in Watson and Raynor's famous experiment with Albert, aged 11 months. Albert was introduced to a variety of animals — including white rats — to demonstrate that an innate fear response to them did not exist. Then, in the presence of a white rat, a loud noise was presented to Albert. A metal bar was hit with a hammer close behind him. He started and fell sideways. This sudden loud noise was repeated a number of times just as the rat was placed in his play pen. The noise was an unconditioned stimulus for fear, and the rat became a conditioned stimulus. After this training, the rat was presented without the noise and Albert responded by crying and crawling away from the rat. A fear response had been conditioned to a new stimulus. According to Watson, such conditioning accounts for all of our emotional responses.

All knowledge, too, is acquired through conditioning. Any statement is a sequence of words, with each word serving as a conditioned stimulus for the next one. When a question is asked, the question serves as a stimulus for the correct answer, a response learned through conditioning.

Watson's primary contributions to psychology were his rejection of the distinction between mind and body, his emphasis on the study of overt behavior, and the thesis that behavior which seemed to be the product of mental activity could be explained in other ways. His influence was so great that most learning theories which followed were behavioristic. Common to all of them is the concern with objectivism, a strong interest in animal studies, a preference for stimulus-response analysis, and a focus on learning as the central problem in psychology.

Watson was not highly thorough in dealing with problems of learning and he had little data to defend his view. Actually, he was not as interested in theory building as with applied psychology and his theory suffered from lack of logical thoroughness. In any event, Watson's influence was profound and even though few today would accept his specific position, scientific psychology is distinctly behavioral.

Skinner and Operant Conditioning

One of the most influential positions regarding the nature of psychology and how it can be applied to education is exemplified by the work of B. F. Skinner. Skinner's system probably represents the most complete and systematic statement of the associationist, behaviorist, environmentalist, determinist position in psychology today.

Because of his preoccupation with strict scientific controls, Skinner has performed most of his experiments with lower animals — principally the pigeon and the white rat. He developed what has become known as the "Skinner box" as a suitable device for animal study. Typically, a rat is placed in a closed box which contains only a lever and a food dispenser. When the rat presses the lever under the conditions established by the experimenter, a food pellet drops into the food tray, thus rewarding the rat. Once the rat has acquired this response, the experimenter can bring the rat's behavior under the control of a variety of stimulus conditions. Furthermore, behavior can be gradually modified or shaped until new responses not ordinarily in the rat's behavioral repertory appear. Success in these endeavors has led Skinner to believe that the laws of learning apply to all organisms. In schools the behavior of pupils may be shaped by careful sequencing of materials and by the presentation of appropriate rewards or reinforcers. Programed learning and teaching machines are the most appropriate means of accomplishing school learning. What is common to man, pigeons, and rats is a world in which certain contingencies of reinforcements prevail.

Skinner established himself as one of the country's leading behaviorists with the publication of his *Behavior of Organisms* in 1938.[1] Although obviously influenced by Watson's behaviorism, Skinner's system appears to follow primarily from the work of Pavlov and Thorndike. Unlike some other followers of Watson, who studied behavior in order to understand the "workings of the mind," Skinner restricted himself to the study of overt or measurable behavior. Without denying either mental or physiological processes, he finds that a study of behavior does not depend on conclusions about what is going on inside the organism.

Every science, he points out, has looked for causes of action inside the things it has studied. Although the practice has proved useful at times, the problem is that events which are located inside a system are likely to be difficult to observe. We are inclined to provide inner explanations without justification and invent causes without fear of contradiction. It is especially tempting to attribute human behavior to the behavior of some inner agent.

Because we have for so long looked inside the organism for an explanation of behavior, we have neglected the variables which are immediately available for a scientific analysis. These variables lie outside the organism. They are found in its immediate environment or in its environmental history. Many of the variables or stimuli are measurable and controllable and, consequently, they make it possible to explain behavior as other subjects are explained in science.

It is evident that the methods of science have been highly successful. Skinner believes that the methods of science should be applied to the field of human affairs. We are all controlled by the world, part of which is constructed by men. Is this control to occur by accident, by tyrants, or by ourselves? A scientific society should reject accidental manipulation. He asserts that a specific plan is needed to promote fully the development of man and society. We cannot make wise decisions if we continue to pretend that we are not controlled.

As Skinner points out, the possibility of behavioral control is offensive to many people. We have traditionally regarded man as a free agent whose behavior occurs by virtue of spontaneous inner changes. We are reluctant to abandon the internal "will" which makes prediction and control of behavior impossible.

Science is an attempt to discover order, to show that certain events stand in lawful relation to other events. For Skinner, order is a working assumption which must be adopted at the very start. We cannot apply the methods of science to human behavior if it is assumed to move about capriciously. Science not only describes, it predicts, and to the extent that relevant conditions can be altered, or otherwise controlled, the future can be controlled. We must assume that behavior is lawful and determined if we are to use the methods of science in the field of human affairs. What a man does is the result of specifiable conditions and once these conditions have been discovered, we can predict and to some extent determine his actions.

Behavior is a difficult subject matter, Skinner says, because it is highly complex and because it is a process, rather than a thing. Although it is changing, fluid, evanescent, and therefore more difficult to study, there is nothing insolvable about the problems which confront the behavioral scientist. A sense of order emerges from any sustained observations of behavior. We make predictions about the behaviors of those with whom we are familiar with a rather high degree of accuracy. If there was no order or uniformity of behavior, we would be ineffective in dealing with one another. A behavioral science is designed to clarify the uniformities in human behavior and to make them explicit.

> We are concerned with the causes of behavior. We want to know why men behave as they do. Any condition or event which can be shown to have an effect upon behavior must be taken into account. By discovering and analyzing these causes we can predict behavior; to the extent that we can manipulate them, we can control behavior."[2]

Skinner notes that a scientific conception of human behavior dictates one practice and a philosophy of personal freedom another. Until we adopt a consistent view we are likely to remain ineffective in solving our social problems. A scientific conception entails the acceptance of an assumption of determinism, the doctrine that behavior is caused and that the behavior which appears is the only one which could have appeared.

Yet the conception that we are free, responsible individuals pervades our practices, codes, and beliefs. A scientific formulation is new and strange and very few people have any notion of the extent to which a science of human behavior is indeed possible.

Society's practices do not represent any clearly defined position. Sometimes we appear to accept man's behavior as spontaneous and responsible, and at other times we recognize that inner determination is not complete and that the individual should not be held accountable. We see the common man as the product of his environment; yet, we give personal credit to great men for their accomplishments. We are in transition. We have not been able to abandon our traditional view of human nature; yet at the same time we are far from clearly adopting a scientific one. In part, we have accepted the assumption of determinism but we easily return to the traditional view when personal aspirations so move us.

For Skinner, then, psychology's task is the prediction and control of behavior and he sees a behavioral technology emerging. As he points out, "Science is steadily increasing our power to influence, change, mold — in a word, control — human behavior. It has extended our understanding . . . so that we deal more successfully with people in nonscientific ways, but it has also identified conditions or variables which can be used to predict and control behavior in a new, and increasingly rigorous, technology."[3] Since all men control and are controlled, control must be analyzed and considered in its proper proportions. Unwarranted fear of control, Skinner believes, had led to the blind rejection of intelligent planning for a better way of life. Since a science of behavior will continue to increase the effective use of control, it is important to understand the processes involved and to prepare for the problems which will arise.

In the following chapter we will examine Skinner's account of learning, or conditioning as he calls it, and how stimulus control of behavior is established.

CHAPTER 4

The Process of Learning: Skinner's Scientific Analysis of Behavior

About all of the behaviors we can identify fall into one of two classes. One which has been called "reflex" or "involuntary" behavior by others is labeled *respondent behavior* by Skinner. The other, usually thought of as "voluntary" behavior, is called *operant behavior* in Skinnner's system. The unscientific nature or ambiguity of meaning of the words "reflex" and "voluntary" led Skinner to rename and define these terms carefully.

Respondent (reflex) behavior takes in all of those responses of human beings, and many other organisms, that are *elicited,* or drawn out, by special stimulus changes in the environment. Some respondents are dilation and contraction of the pupils of your eyes in response to changes in lighting, goose pimples when a cold gust of air touches your skin, shedding a tear when something gets in your eye, perspiration when you find yourself in an overheated room. All of those behaviors that may be identified and labeled as "reflexive" provide examples of respondents.

A second kind of behavior includes a much greater number of human responses. In fact, most human behavior is operant in character. Walking, writing, driving a car, hitting a golf ball show little of respondent character. Operant behavior takes in all of the things we do that have an effect on, or operates on, our outside world. When a child reaches for a cookie, or raises his hand in the classroom, or writes a composition, or solves a math problem, his actions are having some effect on his environment.

Whereas respondents are elicited automatically by a specific class of stimuli from the very beginning, operants are neither automatic nor related to known stimuli. We have no way of knowing initially what will cause an infant to pull himself up to a standing position or to take his first step. There are no special stimuli we can use to evoke these behaviors. We simply must wait for them to occur. For this reason operant behavior is described as *emitted* instead of elicited. We need not be concerned as to what stimuli led to the response.

Two Kinds of Learning

For each kind of behavior, Skinner identifies a type of learning or *conditioning*. Associated with respondent behavior is *respondent conditioning*. Pavlovian, or classical, conditioning is said to be of this sort. As you recall, a new stimulus is paired with the one that already elicits the response, and after a number of pairings the new stimulus comes to elicit the response. A particular stimulus consistently elicits the response. In general, Skinner believes this kind of conditioning plays little part in most human behavior, and he had little concern with it.

The second type of learning Skinner calls *operant conditioning*. Whereas respondent behavior is controlled by a preceding stimulus, operant behavior is controlled by its consequences — stimuli which follow the response.

An infant accidentally touches an object near him in his crib and a tinkling bell-sound comes forth. The infant may look toward the source of the sound momentarily. Later, by chance perhaps, he again brushes his hand against the toy and the bell tinkles. In time we observe that he touches the toy with increasing frequency and looks at it. In this simple example we see illustrated the process of operant conditioning and the very important principle which Thorndike called the Law of Effect and Skinner calls *reinforcement*. It is through this conditioning process (we refer to as learning) that Skinner believes most behavior is acquired.

The events or stimuli which follow a response which tend to strengthen behavior or increase the probability of that response are called *reinforcers*. Any stimulus is a reinforcer if it increases the probability of a response. The response, in our example, was that of touching the toy; the strengthening of the response was seen in its increased frequency of appearance; and the consequence of the response or reinforcer was, of course, the ringing of the bell. We only know that it is a reinforcer because it increased the response of touching the toy.

It is obvious that a response which has *already* occurred cannot be predicted or controlled. It can only be predicted that *similar* responses will be emitted in the future. Therefore when a response is emitted and reinforced, the consequences increase the probability of a *class* of responses. This class of responses is called an *operant*. Rising from a chair, for example, can be accomplished in a variety of ways. A single instance of rising from a chair is a response, but the behavior called "rising from a chair" is an operant. Similarly, eating can have considerable variability in performance, depending on what and where one is eating. This distinction between responses and operants is important, as you will see later in our discussion of modification of behavior.

The effect of your operant behavior on the outside world is often immediate and explicit as it is when you kick a ball, strike a chord on the piano, or stick a pin in a balloon. The consequences of these behaviors may be observed by almost anyone. But this is not always the case. How do we explain behavior when the consequences are not apparent—such as your behavior of asking a student a question when you get no answer, or talking to yourself? In order to explain the acquisition of this or any kind of behavior it is necessary to consider its development. Originally, this behavior did make something happen in the outside world. When you asked a question, someone answered you. Before you started talking to yourself, what you said had some effect on others. The operant behavior would never have been acquired had there been no observable consequences—reinforcers—provided by the world around you.

From our illustration of operant conditioning of the infant, we might raise a question about the toy as a stimulus. How does it differ from a conditioned stimulus which elicits a response in respondent conditioning?

Most operants do acquire a relation to some previous stimuli (called discriminated stimuli); but this relationship is quite different from that found in classical conditioning. We say that the behavior has come under stimulus control. The prior stimulus becomes the *occasion* for the operant behavior, but it is not an eliciting stimulus as in the case of reflexes. A doorknob does not *make* you reach out and turn it; a light switch having become a discriminated stimulus is related to your operant response of moving it, but it is not a reflexive response. We learn to recognize some verbal statements as questions —the voice is raised at the end of the sentence. Such interrogatory verbalizations become discriminated stimuli for some response on our part—it is rude to ignore a question, for that matter. But the question does not elicit a response in us. It is simply the occasion for one and the variability of response or even the absence of one indicates that the behavior is not reflexive.

Although operant behavior is brought under the control of stimuli, such control is only partial and conditional. The operant response of lifting your fork to eat is not simply elicited by the sight of food on your plate. It also depends on such things as hunger, food preferences, whether others have been served, and a variety of other stimulus conditions. For this reason Skinner does not consider it useful to think of operant behavior in terms of specific stimulus-response connections in the sense that respondent behavior is. He sees the behavior as *emitted* by the organism for a variety of reasons or by a multitude of stimuli, most of which are unknown.

Some behavior, such as the crying of a child, can be either respondent or operant. Crying seems to be respondent behavior when it is evoked by stimuli arising from loss of support or from a loud noise. However, if crying is altered when followed by food or other reinforcement provided by the infant's parents, it is operant in nature. If a parent waits until a child's crying reaches a certain intensity, loud crying is more likely to appear in the future. Operant crying depends on its effect on the parents and is maintained or changed according to their response to it. This is not true of respondent crying.

Superstitious Behavior

The power of a single reinforcement is well illustrated in the development of what Skinner calls superstitious behavior. One reinforcement is sufficient to produce a number of operant responses. After receiving a single pellet of food following one response, a rat may respond 50 or more times without the necessity of additional reinforcements to maintain it.

If there is only an accidental connection between the response and the appearance of a reinforcer, the behavior is called "superstitious." ... Suppose we gave a pigeon a small amount of food every fifteen seconds regardless of what it is doing. When food is first given, the pigeon will be behaving in some way—if only standing still—and conditioning will take place. It is then more probable that the same behavior will be in progress when the food is given again. If this proves to be the case, the "operant" will be further strengthened. If not, some other behavior will be strengthened. Eventually a given bit of behavior reaches a frequency at which it is often reinforced. It then becomes a permanent part of the repertoire of the bird, even though the food has been given by a clock which is unrelated to the bird's behavior.

If, for example, three reinforcements were always required in order to change the probability of a response, superstitious behavior would be unlikely. It is only because organisms have reached the point at which a single contingency makes a substantial change that they are vulnerable to coincidences.[1]

It is interesting to consider some of our superstitions in light of this explanation. Many of the rituals we see exhibited on the baseball field or basketball court suggest superstitious behavior. Watch the pitcher's movements before approaching the mound for a pitch or the basketball player's actions as he prepares for a free throw. Just as the knight in armor wore a kerchief from an admiring lady when he charged with his lance, many of us wear a certain shirt or pair of shoes because they "brought us luck." Similarly, we carry charms or place statues on the dashboard of the car often because their presence has accompanied our successes or avoidance of failure. The consequences of these actions serve to confirm our superstitions.

Positive and Negative Reinforcers

The stimuli that happen to act as reinforcers fall into two classes, *positive* and *negative reinforcers*. A positive reinforcer is a stimulus which, when presented, acts to strengthen the behavior that it follows.

If we provide a stimulus such as a cookie following a child's response of saying or attempting to say the word "cookie," and the child says the word more frequently, we have identified that a cookie was a reinforcer for the verbal response. When we call on a student when he raises his hand and see that hand-raising increases in frequency, we suspect that calling on him is presenting him with a positive reinforcer.

The layman usually thinks of a positive reinforcer as a reward but for very good reasons psychologists have avoided the word reward. The word reward implies meaning that the term reinforcer does not. For example, it is difficult to think of a frown from a teacher as a reward; most teachers would not use it for one; yet it could well act as a positive reinforcer for a given child. If it *increases* the frequency of the response the teacher actually hoped to lower by her frown, it is considered a positive reinforcer.

A stimulus such as food may be a reinforcer at one time, when a person has been deprived of food, and not another, when he is *satiated*. The important thing about this definition of reinforcer is that the reinforcing properties do not lie in the stimulus, but in its effect upon behavior. It is evident, then, that reinforcers are relative to the individual and within one individual from time to time. Eating a turkey sandwich does not have the same reinforcing effect after a Thanksgiving dinner that it would have several hours later.

There are negative, as well as positive, reinforcers that may be used to condition operant behavior. Some stimuli by their nature strengthen responses through their removal. When you take off your shoe to remove a stone, when barefoot you jump from a hot sidewalk to the grass, when you cover your ears to cut out loud sounds — in all these instances, you are reinforced by getting rid of stimulation. This is called *escape* behavior.

The kind of stimuli we call unpleasant, annoying, or *aversive* are not distinguished by any particular physical properties. Loud noises, very bright lights, extreme heat or cold, electric shock are quite commonly aversive to people. But for the most part aversive stimuli are relative to individuals and to situations.

Extinction

Of major concern to most of us is that of getting rid of already conditioned behavior. How do we "unlearn" or eliminate a behavior? Although this is quite complex, the rule is simple. The response which occurs repeatedly in the absence of reinforcement will extinguish. When reinforcement is no longer forthcoming, a response becomes less and less frequent. If we quit smoking, we reach less and less often into the pocket that held cigarettes. If television shows become worse, we watch less frequently. If the teacher fails repeatedly to call on a child in class, his hand-raising diminishes in frequency.

If reinforcement is withheld for the purpose of eliminating or weakening a response, it will ultimately in most cases return to its original unconditioned rate (sometimes called the operant level). The failure of a response to be reinforced leads not only to extinction but also to a reaction commonly called frustration. It may become the occasion for considerable emotional expression. Most of us have experienced the failure to start our car on a cold morning. As we persist without success our frustration and even rage mount, but eventually our behavior extinguishes and we try an alternate response — such as calling the service station.

Extinction for both operants and respondents is sometimes very slow to take place. In experimental situations the reinforcer being used is known to the experimenter. In everyday life, however, it is not always easy to identify what may be serving to reinforce a response. Teachers and parents are understandably puzzled at a child's behavior at times because it is not possible to see what is maintaining it — i.e., what the reinforcement is.

If only a few responses have been reinforced, extinction occurs quickly. A long history of reinforcement, on the other hand, leads to a strong resistance to extinction.

Another agent in generating a great resistance to extinction is the schedule of reinforcement that had previously been in effect.

Schedules of Reinforcement

The reinforcement of operant behavior in everyday life does not follow a consistent pattern. The bowler does not attain a "strike" on every attempt; the fisherman does not hook a fish every time he casts his line; and a student does not always answer correctly.

If we only occasionally reinforce a child for good behavior, the behavior is sustained after we discontinue reinforcement much longer than if we had continued to reinforce every response up to the same total number of reinforcements.

Skinner has explored intensively two main classes of intermittent (sometimes called partial) reinforcement: *ratio* and *interval* reinforcement. Ratio reinforcement is based on the number of responses and interval means reinforcement given at intervals of time.

A behavior is usually established by reinforcing each occurrence of the responses—a continuous schedule of reinforcement. Once it has been conditioned, however, it is not the most economical way to *maintain* behavior. Having been conditioned, behavior may usually be maintained by only an occasional or intermittent reinforcer.

Behavior can be reinforced intermittently according to a number of different schedules. Reinforcement may be provided in terms of the number of responses emitted (ratio schedules) or in terms of the passage of time (interval schedules) or in combinations of the two. For example, if the schedule is a "fixed ratio 10," then each tenth response is reinforced: reinforcement is provided only after ten responses have been emitted.

Such ratio schedules may be *fixed*, as in the previous example, or they may be *variable*. Under a variable ratio schedule, the number of responses required for reinforcement varies about some mean or average. Sometimes reinforcement follows five responses and sometimes as many as thirty responses may be required before reinforcement is forthcoming.

Schedules based primarily on the passage of time are called *interval schedules*. The interval is fixed when a constant interval of time must elapse between reinforcements. We may arrange conditions so that an interval of five minutes must elapse before the next response is reinforced. On a variable interval schedule, the length of time varies about some given mean time.

There are certain characteristics of responding on each basic schedule which have been found in studies of many species of animals, including man. The characteristics of a great many schedules that were first established in lower animals have generally been found to produce similar results in studies of normal, retarded and autistic children, and normal and psychotic adults.

Ratio schedules are characterized by a high rate of responding because the more rapidly the person responds, the sooner reinforcement occurs. A man who offers to paint your house for a fixed amount of money, as opposed to charging you by the hour, has placed himself on a fixed ratio. Factory piecework in which payment depends directly on the number of items produced is another example of a ratio schedule. In school assignments in reading of a given number of pages, in arithmetic of a set number of problems, or in physical education a specified number of situps and pushups are provided illustrations of fixed ratio performances. In fixed ratio reinforcement schedules, although the rate of responding is relatively high, there tends to be a period of inactivity following reinforcement.

When the ratio is variable, an even higher rate of responding is found. Most gambling, and notably playing slot machines, is seen as variable ratio reinforcement. The inveterate gambler requires only an occasional win to sustain his behavior. However, extinction following conditioning on ratio schedules usually occurs in a relatively short period of time. When the gambler feeds the slot machine at a high rate without a win, his behavior quickly extinguishes.

On interval schedules, where reinforcement depends on the passage of time, the overall rate of responding is low. There is no reason to work rapidly, since reinforcement will not occur until a given point in time. If the interval is fixed—as in the assignment of a term paper at the end of the semester—there is a low rate of responding at the beginning of the period with a gradual increase to a very high rate.

When a teacher gives examinations at three- or six-week intervals he or she should expect a rather low rate of responding—less studying —following an examination and a rather high rate just before the exam. We sometimes call this "cramming." On the other hand, unannounced exams or "pop quizzes" are on a variable interval schedule and produce sustained responding at a low rate. The longer the interval between tests and reinforcements the lower the rate of responding.

Extinction following interval schedules is characterized by a low sustained rate that gradually tapers off. So if the number of reinforcements is held constant these schedules produce the most enduring behavior. If one wants the behavior to last a long time after reinforcement is discontinued, interval schedules are most appropriate. This also accounts for the difficulty, very likely, of extinguishing some behaviors we would prefer to see disappear. Inconsistency on the part of parents or teachers in dispensing reinforcers suggests a variable schedule that fosters persistency at times when it is not the goal. If unwanted behavior, like whining or crying to have what he wants, only occasionally succeeds for the child, the response is likely to be maintained even when scolding is sometimes the consequence of his behavior.

Primary and Secondary Reinforcers

Food, water, and sexual contact, as well as escapes from injurious conditions, are called primary reinforcers because they are obviously connected with the well-being of the organism, i.e., they have biological significance. They play a major role in the acquisition and maintenance of certain classes of behaviors—including escape and avoidance. Touching a hot stove, grabbing a bumble bee, staying in the summer sun too long—all serve to illustrate the modifying influence of negative reinforcers which arise naturally from one's behaviors.

But other events are reinforcing to the human being. Some forms of stimulation are positively reinforcing, although they do not appear to be related to behavior having survival value. A baby shakes a rattle, a child explores his mother's closet, a boy flies a kite, a musician plays his violin. Some auditory, tactical, visual stimuli, it may be argued, are naturally reinforcing in the sense that a capacity to be reinforced by any feedback from the environment would be biologically advantageous. It is important, however, to consider the possibility that in some cases the reinforcing effect is *conditioned*—that the reinforcers themselves are "learned."

We rarely see conditioning, especially at the human level, in which primary reinforcers are involved. Much more characteristic in operant conditioning involving human subjects are secondary or *conditioned reinforcers*. We are more often conditioned by contrived reinforcers presented by others, such as their approval or disapproval, or promises or threats, or by being told we are right or wrong.

Skinner has demonstrated that if each time a light is turned on when a hungry pigeon is given food, the light eventually becomes a conditioned reinforcer. It may then be used to condition operant behavior just as food is used. The more often the light is paired with food, the more reinforcing it becomes, but this power is rapidly lost when all food is withheld. The reader may, of course, recognize this as Pavlovian or respondent conditioning.

One of the important properties of conditioned reinforcers is that they sustain behavior until an ultimate primary reinforcement is forthcoming. Many human activities are characterized by long delays before primary reinforcement is achieved. e.g., attending college, planting a vegetable garden, building a football team. If it were not for interim conditioned reinforcers to provide encouragement, there would be little to sustain our behavior. Often we supply ourselves these reinforcements.

So too, respondent or classical conditioning seems to apply to the function of negative reinforcement. Neutral stimuli which accompany or precede established negative reinforcements become themselves negatively reinforcing. The sound and sight of the dentist's drill, the burning of a fuse on a firecracker, the raising of a fist—all serve to illustrate conditioned negative reinforcers. As a result of these conditioned reinforcers, we move to escape from the aversive stimuli even though they have not yet occurred.

These conditioned negative reinforcers are used in many ways. We shame people into acting in socially appropriate ways. We warn and threaten young people by pairing certain acts with certain consequences, such as the relationship of sexual behavior to pregnancy or venereal disease.

Generalized Reinforcers

A conditioned reinforcer becomes generalized when it has been paired with more than one primary reinforcer. When we reinforce with food, we achieve control only over the hungry organism. Generalized reinforcers are useful because the momentary condition of the organism is less important. Money is an effective generalized reinforcer because it can reinforce a great variety of behaviors under various conditions.

Attention, approval, and affection are particularly notable as generalized reinforcers. Before we can receive other reinforcements from someone, we must first have him pay attention to us. When a child exhibits "attention-getting behavior," he is more apt to receive the attention of that person who can supply other reinforcements. Another person is likely to reinforce only the behaviors of which he approves.

Signs of approval, then, become reinforcing. We use verbal responses like "good," "that's right," "I like that" to shape the behavior of others. Equally reinforcing may be the non-verbal signs like a smile, the pat on the back, the affirmative nod.

One of the most powerful of the generalized reinforcers which we use to modify the behaviors of others is affection. It is so important to us that it is often spoken of as if it were a primary reinforcer. Effective as it is as a reinforcer, it is easy to assume an inherent "need for affection." But then one could build a similar rationale for the "need for money," also a powerful generalized reinforcer.

Eventually generalized reinforcers are effective even though the primary reinforcers upon which they are based no longer accompany them.

Avoidance

Escaping from an aversive situation is clearly not the same as avoiding one. If a response terminates ongoing aversive conditions, it is escape behavior. In avoiding aversive stimulation we are responding to conditioned stimuli which postpone the onset of aversive stimulation. For example, for a number of reasons a young boy may cry and try to avoid getting his hair cut by a barber. Let us assume for the moment that on the occasion of his first haircut the barber accidentally pinched his neck. At the time this aversive stimulus was presented other stimuli such as the barber's white jacket, the sight and sound of the electric clippers, the physical features of the barber shop were observable. Since these stimuli were present just prior to and at the onset of the aversive stimulus, these neutral stimuli acquire aversive properties through stimulus substitution. When he escapes from the situation, his response is strengthened through operant conditioning. On subsequent occasions he may respond to the conditioned stimuli such as the sound of the clippers, the sight of the barber shop, or even the mention of a haircut by the parents. By crying or otherwise trying to avoid the haircut, he may succeed in avoiding all aversive stimulation. But an interesting thing happens. The escape response to conditioned stimuli weakens upon repeated occasions; it gradually extinguishes because the behavior has not been reinforced by the aversive stimulus — the pinch. His crying and wriggling in the barber's chair diminishes to an occasional whimper, which eventually is not emitted and extinction has occurred. Hopefully, the primary reinforcer is not received again, for if it is, a single instance may suffice to recondition the reinforcing power of the neutral stimuli.

It would seem that much of our day-to-day behavior is avoidance. We pay taxes, we diet, we obey traffic rules, we spray our gardens with poisons, we study for examinations more to avoid negative consequences, perhaps, than to produce positive ones. These behaviors are important to us in successfully avoiding unfavorable consequences. However, in operant conditioning the basic rule applies.

The withholding of reinforcement following a response leads to extinction. If an aversive situation is always avoided, the threat grows weaker and the behavior is less and less strongly reinforced. Eventually we fail to emit the avoidance response, and aversive stimulation follows. We run through a red light or drive too fast and receive a traffic citation and fine. The conditioned reinforcers are then reestablished as negative reinforcers. Similarly "empty threats" by parents and teachers soon lose their effectiveness because the child or student sees that negative reinforcers do not follow and "obeying responses" extinguish.

In the following vignette consider the escape and avoidance responses conditioned through negative reinforcement. Notice that the effect of reinforcement, either positive or negative, is always to increase the probability of that response. How might extinction be facilitated?

Tom, on his first day at the new school, falls on the playground and skins his elbow. He starts to cry and another boy who turns out to be the school "bully" teases him for crying. The other children laugh. Later in the classroom the teacher calls on Tom to read. He has trouble with one of the first big words he comes to. The teacher frowns and calls on another student. Tom's stomach begins to hurt. He gets permission from the teacher to go home early. He feels better as he leaves the school. The next day Tom tells his mother he does not feel well enough to go to school.

Thus far our discussion has dwelt principally with rate or frequency of responding. In addition to the frequency of a behavior, however, we are very much concerned with the conditions under which responses occur, the quality or appropriateness of a behavior. Skinner approaches this problem, at least in part, through his analysis of induction or generalization, discrimination of stimuli, and differentiation of response.

For our purposes we may distinguish between stimulus generalization, stimulus discrimination, response generalization, and response differentiation. It should be recognized, however, that for explanatory purposes this is an arbitrary classification of events which are seldom clearly separated in everyday behavior.

Stimulus Generalization

Earlier it was pointed out that previous stimuli do become functionally related to operants. Although they do not elicit them, they become the occasion for responses. When behavior has thus been brought under control of a given stimulus, we find that other similar stimuli are also effective. This spread of effect to other stimuli is called generalization or induction. The fact that this occurs points out that any given stimulus may possess a number of values or properties which may be separately effective. As Skinner illustrates:

> If we reinforce a response (made by a pigeon, for example) to a round, red spot one square inch in area, a yellow spot of the same size and shape will be effective because of the common properties of size and shapes; a square, red spot of the same area will be effective because of its color and size; and a round, red spot half an inch in area will be effective because of the common properties of color and shape.[2]

Induction is not an activity of the organism but rather a term indicating that the control acquired by a stimulus is shared by other stimuli with common properties. Any stimulus, then, is comprised of a particular combination of properties, any aspect of which may exercise control over behavior. Stimulus generalization may be accounted for when we can identify the common properties of two stimuli.

For example, a rather wide range of hues evoke the response "red." The word "red" is adequate in most everyday situations even though we may recognize that there is considerable variability in the stimuli we call red. Some common property is shared by the different stimuli and it is this characteristic responsible for our mutual response.

Our "mistakes" are often accounted for by stimulus generalizations. We may respond in a way that seemed quite appropriate at the time, only to sense later that our response was based on elements of the situation which misguided our behavior in the current circumstance. We may wave to a friend only to find out it was a stranger who is in some way similar. The "ambiguity" of a teacher's question which leads to an "incorrect" response on the part of a student provides an example. There are a number of appropriate answers to the question "How do you get from Chicago to New York?" If the student answers "by airplane," and teacher expects the answer "move in an easterly direction," she may consider the answer wrong or that the student is "acting smart."

The survival value of generalizations to organisms seems evident. Many of us, for instance, respond similarly to a variety of snakes. In doing so we make "mistakes," but such generalization has prevented contact with those that are potentially dangerous to us.

Stimulus Discrimination

If generalization was always the rule, our behavior would be highly confusing. Any behavior might be likely to occur in any situation. We learn *not* to generalize; we learn to make a given response only in the presence of certain stimuli and other stimuli are no longer the occasion for the response. Discrimination is accomplished by reinforcing behavior in the presence of one stimulus (or group of stimuli) and not reinforcing it in other stimulus situations. When the child says "dog" in the presence of a dog, his parents reinforce his behavior. Saying "dog" in the presence of inappropriate objects such as a horse is not reinforced and eventually the child says "dog" in the presence of dogs and not in the presence of other objects. He has learned to discriminate and to make a differential response.

As you can see, discrimination plays a very important role in our understanding of "learning." Many thousands of discriminations must be made by each of us in meeting the requirements of the world around us. Operant behavior, for which we could identify no eliciting stimulus at the beginning, later comes to be almost completely under the control of stimuli. It does so because we have provided reinforcements in the presence of appropriate stimuli and have withheld it in the presence of others. The choir director lifts one finger, a hundred eyes follow this movement, and together the voices respond appropriately. A traffic light turns from red to green and the discrimination leads to a differential response. A child learns to say "bee" to the letter "b" and inhibits this response to "d", which would tend perhaps to generalize due to the similarity of stimuli.

Thus, we see that even though a person responds in the same way to similar situations, generalization continues only if the responses are reinforced in the new situation. If the person's response is not reinforced in the new situation, it will extinguish. The response will occur only in situations where it has been reinforced.

Much of our behavior has come under the control of certain stimuli because in the past it has been reinforced in the presence of those stimuli. Some of our behaviors are reinforced in the presence of certain people and they, as stimulus objects, gain control over our behavior. We behave differently in the presence of a close friend or family member than we do in the presence of a teacher or minister. Different responses have been reinforced in their presence.

Many verbal stimuli come to control one's behavior because they have come to be discriminated stimuli. "Do you want a cookie?" has been expressed in the presence of visual stimuli and responses in the presence of these stimuli were reinforced. The response to a request "Please help me" has been followed by expression of gratitude, praise, or other reinforcers. The behaviors occur because in the past, in the presence of these verbal stimuli, the appropriate behavior was reinforced.

The very important behavior we call *abstraction* is a type of discrimination learning. Technically, abstraction describes the process in which a response comes under the control of a single *element* of a stimulus that is common to many stimuli but does not exist apart from those stimuli. Suppose, for example, that a child is reinforced for saying "red" in the presence of a ball. But if he calls a blue or green ball "red," reinforcement does not follow and discriminations begin to form. Because the attributes of redness is reinforced in the presence of many other red objects—a fire engine, a block, a crayon, and non-reinforcement occurs when he calls objects "red" inappropriately, an abstraction for "red" is acquired. The single characteristic which many diverse stimulus objects have in common, "redness," controls the response "red."

Response Generalization

Behavior which is strengthened in one situation is likely to occur in other situations. Training in one area of skilled behavior may improve one's performance in some other area. A child who has been reinforced for sitting and listening quietly while mother is reading is apt to behave similarly in kindergarten or other classroom situations. Having developed the ability to ride a bicycle would appear to facilitate the performance of operating a motorcycle.

This phenomenon, called *response generalization* or response induction or transfer, is a very important one and is given considerable attention in psychological and educational literature. If it were not for generalization each of our behaviors would have to be acquired in each new situation we encounter. Our achievements would be vastly limited because we would be spending so much time in acquisition of new skills and so little on the use of previous acquisitions.

Few question that transfer occurs, but the meaning of the term, the interpretation and implications of the phenomena, involve considerable research and dispute. What is transfer? How can behavior which has not been reinforced directly be strengthened? For Skinner this is a pseudo problem. In reinforcing one operant, a noticeable increase in the strength in another is often produced. He says, "We divide behavior into hard and fast units and are then surprised to find that the organism disregards the boundaries we have set."[3] In explaining transfer he points out that it is difficult to think of any response which does not have something in common with another. The continuous nature of behavior would lead us to this conclusion. The same muscular system may be involved in many activities. If we reinforce the last response in a sequence of responses, we may strengthen all units which contain the same sequence of responses.

Response Differentiation

Since a response must be made before it can be strengthened by reinforcers, it would appear that we are describing behavior that has *already* been learned. Indeed, to Skinner the present probability of response may be of greater interest than how it was first acquired. But we want to know how his system accounts for new, original responses.

In operant conditioning when reinforcement is contingent on the properties of stimuli, it is referred to as discrimination, which we have discussed. When reinforcement is contingent on the properties of the response it is sometimes called *differentiation*. It is through this process and principles now to be discussed that it is possible to "produce" behavior that would not ordinarily occur.

Let us begin by illustrating a behavior of a pigeon described by Skinner.[4] If we saw a pigeon walking around with its head held as high in the air as possible, we would consider it quite unusual. A pigeon can, however, be conditioned to behave in this way. We could wait for such behavior to occur so that it could be reinforced, but we might have a very long wait and conditioning might be somewhat ineffective. The pigeon can be gradually conditioned to perform this response.

As we observe the pigeon in his cage, we see that there are variations in the height he holds his head. If we provide reinforcements only when his head is held high—the extreme variations of normal responding—we find that the behavior of raising his head increases in frequency. As we continue to reinforce only the extreme responses emitted, those that were extreme become more typical. His behavior becomes quite different from that observed at the beginning of this conditioning process.

Several principles can be identified through this example and much of our earlier discussion can be brought into focus.

Behavior normally occurs with some variations. As we pointed out earlier, operants are not individual instances of a response; rather they are a class of similar but variable responses (operants). Reinforcement strengthens all responses in that class, as we saw in response generalization.

Through a series of reinforced approximations of an organism, a rare response can be increased to a very high probability in a short time. If we only reinforce the more extreme responses in the range of responses emitted, the constitution of the class will change in that direction. There will still be variation, but the responses will vary around a new position. Some variations of a response class "differentiate out" and become conditioned, while others in that class are extinguished.

If only those responses which are made in the direction of some desired behavior are reinforced, this class of responses will drift in this direction. When subsequent responses are emitted that are even more like the behavior wanted, they are reinforced again and again and the class of responses gradually shifts in that direction. If this is done in a gradually increasing manner, the organism is conditioned to behave in a very extreme way which would not otherwise have occurred. A series of differentiations of this nature is called *shaping*, or the method of *successive approximations*.

The task of shaping behavior requires considerable skill as can be seen from Reese's description:

> Since the reinforced response is the one that immediately precedes reinforcement, it is important to reinforce the desired behavior quickly, before another response intervenes. . . . As new approximations are reached and reinforced, earlier ones are extinguished. If we progress too slowly, the subject may satiate, or a given approximation may become so firmly established that there is little chance for other responses to occur. If we progress too rapidly, demanding an approximation that is not yet likely to occur, the behavior we have shaped will begin to extinguish, and we will have to backtrack to an earlier approximation and work up again.

> Skillful shaping consists of selecting the right responses to reinforce and in knowing how long to reinforce each approximation before moving on to the next. Since reinforcement must be delivered immediately, there is not time to wait for a response to occur and then decide whether or not to reinforce it. The experimenter (or animal trainer or teacher or parent) has to *anticipate* the response in order to be able to reinforce it immediately. He has to predict the behavior before he can control it. He has to know what behavior is likely to occur under what conditions, and the only way to do this is to know his subject very well.[5]

It is not difficult to find illustrations of the principles of shaping in everyday life. Children playing hide-the-thimble utilize the shaping process when they call out "you're getting warmer" as the one seeking the thimble makes a move in the direction of the hiding place. Reinforcements in the form of "feedback" increase the frequency of movements followed by the reinforcer.

The operation of the principles of differentiation and successive approximation are not limited to extreme behaviors. Although they are more dramatically illustrated in such cases, they are equally important in shaping behavior we call "normal." Most of our behaviors which have been reinforced by parents, teachers, and peers shape our responses in the direction of the mean rather than the extreme. The development of language proceeds by successive approximations which have been reinforced. If we waited for perfect articulation of a word before reinforcing a child, he might never acquire adequate language skills. If a coach waited until his football team had a perfect season before providing reinforcements, it is doubtful that they would ever achieve this objective. The gradual change brought about by reinforcement of successive approximations is a continual shaping process. The behavior we observe has been continuously modified from a basic repertoire which was largely undifferentiated. Skinner sees shaping behavior as analogous to a sculptor shaping a lump of clay. "At no point does anything emerge which is very different from what preceded it. . . . We cannot find a point at which it suddenly appears."[6]

The immediacy of reinforcement is critical in conditioning, otherwise the precision of the differential effect is lost. This is one of the major difficulties in traditional classroom teaching, where the teacher is attempting to be responsive to the behaviors of perhaps 30 students.

Reinforcement is provided not only by consequences which we contrive; natural reinforcers in the form of feedback from the outside world and from our body movements shape our behavior in many instances. They are most likely to satisfy the criterion of immediacy of reinforcement. For example, by the reinforcement of slightly exceptional instances of his behavior a child learns to roll over, to sit up, to stand, to crawl, and eventually to walk. Such changes of behavior do not depend predominantly on changes in the external world. There are fewer outside clues to tell him when reinforcement is available and when it is not. Rather, the feedback is provided from the movement itself rather than from an external source.

To a considerable extent good form in golf or in bowling is developed and maintained by feedback of this sort. It is evident, however, that the effects of behavior upon a golf ball or bowling pins are needed to maintain the reinforcing power of bodily feedback.

In other instances reinforcement may be supplied relatively automatically by the environment. As the car slows down going up a hill, we press down on the accelerator. When a student in the back row indicates he cannot hear, we speak louder. In playing an instrument important differences in the consequences, such as vibrato in a violin, rest on fine differences in our behavior. Negative reinforcers are also important in the refinement of skills. For example the consequences which are involved in conditioning of walking, climbing stairs, or riding a bicycle are to a great extent the avoidance of falls.

Punishment

Earlier we discussed extinction procedures, the non-reinforcement of a response, for eliminating a behavior. Probably the most common method used to eliminate behavior, however, is punishment. Although punishment is a highly complex and controversial subject which has generated considerable research, the intention here is to present Skinner's position: that in the long run, unlike reinforcement, punishment "works to the disadvantage of both the punished organism and the punishing agency."[7]

Ostensibly punishment is used to reduce tendencies to behave in certain ways. We spank and scold children for misbehavior; we fine, lock up, or assign to hard labor adults who break laws; we threaten, censure, disapprove, ostracize, coerce, in our efforts to control social behaviors. Does punishment in fact do what it is supposed to do?

The effects of punishment, it has been found, are not the opposite of reward. It does not subtract responses where reinforcement adds them. Rather it appears to temporarily suppress a behavior and when punishment is discontinued, eventually responses will reappear. But this is only one aspect of the topic. Let us look at it in further detail.

Skinner defines punishment in two ways, first as the withdrawal of a positive reinforcer and, second, as the presentation of a negative reinforcer or aversive stimulus. We take candy away from a child or we spank him. Note that the arrangement in punishment is the opposite of that in reinforcement, where a positive reinforcer is presented and a negative reinforcer is removed.

Since we remove positive reinforcers to extinguish a response and also to punish it, a distinction must be made. When a response is made and no reinforcement follows, i.e., *nothing* happens, the response gradually extinguishes. However, if we *withdraw* a reinforcer and the withdrawal of a reinforcer is contingent on a response, responding is suppressed more rapidly. The latter is punishment. Sometimes we withdraw a privilege from a child to control his behavior. A teacher might keep a child in the classroom during recess or cancel a field trip as a result of misbehavior. Turning off television when a child puts his thumb in his mouth may effectively suppress thumbsucking. Most punishments of this sort utilize conditioned or generalized reinforcers. Quite frequently one sees adults withdraw attention or affection as punishment for misbehavior, sometimes in subtle ways.

Withdrawal of opportunity to obtain reinforcement (called "time out") is used by parents and has been used experimentally to modify behavior. Most often this is done by removing the subject from the reinforcing situation; e.g., "go to your room," "sit in the corner." If the situation from which a child is removed is providing reinforcement, there is presumably motivation to return. However, one of the risks taken in using punishment can be illustrated here. By sending a child from a classroom for misbehavior, we may be reinforcing escape behavior. If his classroom behaviors are not positively reinforced, by and large, leaving the classroom may be reinforced by escape from an aversive situation.

More commonly we think of punishment as the presentation of an aversive stimulus. This need not be administered by another person to effect subsequent behavior. A child who touches a hot stove or who has eaten strawberries to which he is allergic is punished for his behavior.

Most of our information about punishment, for obvious reasons, has been generated by research with non-human subjects — rats, pigeons, monkeys. For this reason and because of the variability and complexity of punishing situations, only tentative principles may be offered. It is highly probable that there are a number of important variables such as severity of punishment, the frequency of its use, and the degree of motivation which influence behavior under punishing conditions.

Punishment seems to suppress responding only temporarily. When punishment stops, responding gradually recovers. If punishment is severe, however, there is very little recovery. In most studies, even with human subjects, if the motivation for punished behavior is strong and if there are no alternative behaviors, the behavior is only temporarily suppressed. When punishment is removed the response returns to its previous strength.

Skinner describes three effects of punishment. The first effect is the suppression of behavior. This seems to occur when one's response to punishment is incompatible with the behavior being punished. Making a child laugh by making funny faces or otherwise distracting him is incompatible with crying but it is not an example of punishment. On the other hand, scolding a child for laughing inappropriately in class leads to responses which are incompatible with laughter and tends to suppress it temporarily.

Punishment is administered, however, with the intention of having more enduring effects. It is anticipated that punishment would not be needed in future situations to control behavior.

The extent to which an undesirable behavior is suppressed without direct control is accounted for through the conditioning of emotional responses, the second effect of punishment. Stimuli which precede and accompany punishment acquire aversive properties themselves. They become conditioned aversive stimuli and their presence suppresses behavior. If a parent says "no-no" and slaps a child's hand, the verbal expression itself becomes aversive through conditioning and suppresses the behavior. Similarly a teacher's frown or other cue suffices to suppress a response in a student because the frown in the past occurred in the presence of punishment. If on later occasions these conditioned aversive stimuli precede punishment by a sufficient length of time to observe changes in behavior, we see results which are called *anxiety*.

Punishment seems always to be accompanied by anxiety. Almost every strong aversive stimulus is preceded by a discriminated stimulus which may generate these emotional responses. Consider your reaction to seeing a train bearing down a track toward a stalled car. One of the problems of anxiety is that it interferes with the normal behavior of the individual and may even prevent appropriate avoidance behavior from occurring. This happens because anxiety includes respondent changes such as increased heart rate, blood pressure, respiration, and muscle tension which explains its far-reaching effects. These respondents are incompatible with most operant behavior and their debilitating effect must be considered as a possible by-product of severe punishment. For example, if sexual behavior is severely punished, the conditioned stimulus gives rise to emotional responses which interfere with the completion of the behavior. However, the punishment and subsequent conditioned stimuli may later interfere with socially acceptable sexual behavior by evoking incompatible respondent behavior and suppressing operant behavior. The emotions aroused under these circumstances are the main ingredients of guilt or shame. Similarly anxiety in test situations can interfere with a student's performance. If tests have been used as threats in the past, tests themselves constitute punishment and are accompanied by respondent changes we call anxiety.

We still have no reason to suppose that the punished behavior has been permanently weakened. It is now merely temporarily suppressed by conditioned stimuli as opposed to the punishment itself.

The third and most important effect of punishment is as follows. Earlier we had noted that mental stimuli acquired aversive properties through a process of stimulus substitution. The sight or sound of a bee is sufficient to produce avoidance behavior. In such a case we are escaping from conditioned aversive stimuli, not the sting of the bee itself, and our behavior is reinforced.

As a child is about to light matches, a behavior for which he was previously punished, aversive conditioned stimuli arising from his behavior (anxiety) and the sight of the matchbook, are generated. Putting the matches away or similar avoidance responses are reinforced because they provide escape from the conditioned aversive stimuli. Further punishment has been avoided.

Now, if punishment in this way is repeatedly avoided, in other words, by escape from conditioned stimuli, the responses to the conditioned aversive stimuli undergo extinction. The incompatible behavior (in our example, that of putting away the matches) is less strongly reinforced and the punished behavior eventually returns. Let us suppose on this occasion he lights a match and burns his finger. Stimuli are reconditioned through the punishment and doing something other than playing with matches is again reinforced. If punishment (burning his finger) does not occur again, as his skills develop in lighting matches, the behavior returns in full strength.

Severe punishment without question has the immediate effect of reducing a particular response. People continue to use punishment for behavioral control for this reason. Another reason which has been offered for the widespread use of punishment is that punishment reinforces the punisher. When a behavior occurs that is aversive to us, such as annoying or rude behavior of a child, we punish it. By our response of punishing, the annoying behavior (aversive stimulus) is removed, constituting negative reinforcement. Even if the suppressed behavior recurs on occasion, or if punishment appears only to work now and then, the intermittent schedule reinforces and sustains the parents' punishing behavior. Most adults believe that punishment is a necessary and effective method of control.

It is Skinner's position, therefore, that in the long run punishment does not actually eliminate a behavior, and the temporary suppression of it is obtained at a tremendous cost in reducing efficiency and happiness. We may avoid the use of punishment by weakening behaviors in other ways. If it is not possible to establish conditions for extinction, i.e., the withholding of reinforcement following the response, conditioning other incompatible behavior through positive reinforcement may eliminate an undesirable behavior. It may well be that temporarily suppressing one response through mild punishment is effective because an alternate response occurs which is then strengthened through positive reinforcers. Direct positive reinforcement is always preferable because it appears to have fewer objectionable by-products.

Chaining

The processes of discrimination and differentiation which we have discussed operate together throughout our lives. As adults we have acquired a vast number of differentiated responses that may be made to an even larger number of discriminated stimuli. We shift skillfully from one response to another as the stimulus patterns which confront us are changed. Behavior in everyday situations appears to be a continuous ongoing sequence, with one response leading smoothly to another. When one response produces or alters the variables which control another response, it is called chaining. Actually, most behavior occurs in chains. Counting or saying the letters of the alphabet are simple illustrations of chains, where the response of saying the first number or letter provides the discriminated stimulus for the second number or letter, and so on.

Chains are not confined to the production of discriminated stimuli, since other variables may be altered by behavior. As we eat our dinners each bite has the usual effect of making the next bite less probable because the condition of deprivation is being changed.

For the most part, however, discriminated stimuli evoke differential responses, which produce further discriminated stimuli and differential responses, which eventually lead to reinforcements.

Keller describes the behavior of a white rate named Pliny which effectively illustrates the end product of conditioning a chain of responses:

He would first pull a string that hung from the top of his cage. This pull would cause a marble to be released from an overhead rack. When the marble fell to the floor, he would pick it up in his forepaws and carry it across the cage to a small tube that projected vertically two inches above the floor. He would then lift the marble to the top of the tube and drop it inside, whereupon a pellet of food was automatically discharged into a nearby tray. Pliny would then approach the tray, seize the pellet, eat it, and turn again to repeat the sequence of acts.[8]

In human behavior, units which may have been quite distinct originally group into larger units, which makes it quite difficult for an observer to identify the different links in a chain.

We tend to think of getting dressed as a relatively simple task but when one attempts to teach this behavior, for example, to a retarded child, its complexity is amplified. We must realize that a sequence of behavior, such as pulling on the trousers, is a chain of responses and may be very difficult for a retarded child to master all at once. By careful analysis of the behavior, bits of behavior to be learned can be identified.

Chains of responses appear to be established in a backward fashion. For instance, the last response to be acquired by Pliny was to pull the string, the first response in the chain. The first link in a sequence is the last one to be added. Where possible, then, it is best to teach long sequences by starting near the *end* of a sequence, teaching the last step first. In pulling on trousers, the trainer helps the child into his trousers so that they are almost on. He is then asked to pull them up. In the beginning, it may be necessary to put his hands on the trousers, to reinforce by touching them or pulling slightly. Closer approximations are required for reinforcement as the behavior is shaped.

In the next step the child is helped again into the trousers but this time they are left farther down on his legs, perhaps below his knees. He is again instructed to pull up his trousers. As the behavior is modified, reinforcement is usually provided only on completion of the full act of pulling the trousers up. If difficulty is encountered, it is necessary to back up and shape more gradually.

In the last phase the trousers are placed in front of him and he is asked to put on his trousers. Attempting to put his feet in the trousers is reinforced, as are other steps in the sequence. Finally as his skill improves in each stage, the total sequence is required before reinforcement is provided. Generally when the skill has been acquired other reinforcements maintain the behavior. Dressing usually is followed by having breakfast and this reinforcement is contingent upon his having dressed himself.

Some type of stimuli involved in chaining are internal to the organism and some are external. Internal stimuli arise from the intestines, glands, muscles. In addition, a response may produce external stimuli; walking brings about the occurrence of new visual stimuli, for example. Talking consists of muscular movements and our vocal response which produces sound stimuli. These auditory stimuli are important in maintaining our sequences of speech responses. Thus, any stimulus that a response produces may come to control the next response in the chain.

Imitation

In spite of strong belief to the contrary, imitative behavior does not appear to arise through any inherent reflex mechanism (for example, the Freudian concept of identification). Imitation develops as the result of discriminative reinforcements. A response is made in the presence of a stimulus and is reinforced.

The behavior of imitating others is so well developed in the average person that we forget its origins and it is easily accepted as an inherent part of his behavior.

Imitation plays an important part in human learning. In the development of language, for example, the child's spontaneous vocalizations that approximate adult language are reinforced. The parent reinforces imitative behavior. We name an object and tell the child to repeat what we have said. When he does so we praise him. Vocabulary, then, is developed—at least in part—by the reinforcement of imitative responses.

Imitation is also encouraged in skill development. We most frequently demonstrate skills to the learner by saying "watch what I do" and "I'll show you." Observing the consequences of other behavior affects the degree to which a model is imitated. (Bandura and Walters[9] have reviewed research in this area.)

Reverse imitation also occurs. We can easily establish behavior in which the imitator does exactly the opposite of the person being imitated (dancing, tennis, fencing). In such cases a response on the part of one individual constitutes a discriminative stimulus for a different response on the part of the other.

Although there is much more that can be said about Skinner's system, and much detail has been omitted, this brings to a close this portion of our discussion. In the chapter which follows we will focus more specifically on the educational implications of the theory.

CHAPTER 5

Implications for Teaching: The Technology of Teaching

There are several notable deficiencies in our present methods of teaching from Skinner's point of view. Advances in our control of the learning process in recent years suggest a thorough revision of classroom practices. Because education affects all of us, it is perhaps the most important branch of scientific technology. Certainly we should focus on ways to improve it, ways that are within our reach.

One of the major problems in teaching, he says, is the use of aversive control. Although some schools still use physical punishment, in general there has been a shift to non-corporal measures such as ridicule, scolding, sarcasm, criticism, extra homework, forced labor, withdrawal of privileges. Examinations are used as threats and are designed to show principally what the student does not know and to coerce him to study. The student spends a great part of his day doing things he does not want to do and for which no positive reinforcements are forthcoming. Consequently, he works mainly to escape aversive stimulation. He does what he has to because the teacher holds the power and authority. But in time the student discovers other ways of escaping. He is tardy or absent, he does not pay attention (thus withdrawing reinforcers from the teacher), he daydreams or is restless, he forgets what he learns, he may become aggressive and refuse to obey, he may drop out when he is legally able to do so.

Skinner believes that most teachers are humane and do not want to use aversive controls. Consequently, they too become unhappy with their plight. Aversive techniques continue to be used, in all probability, because effective alternatives have not been developed.

Children learn without being taught, Skinner says, because they are naturally interested in some activities and learn by themselves. For this reason some educators have advocated the use of the method of discovery. But, says Skinner, discovery is no solution to the problems of education. To be strong a culture must transmit itself; it must impart its accumulation of knowledge, skills, and social and ethical practices to children. The institution of education was established to serve this purpose. Furthermore, great thinkers have built upon the past rather than wasting time rediscovering it. Could we seriously believe that children can discover writing and reading skills, mathematics, genetics? Certainly students should be encouraged to explore, to ask questions, to work and study independently, to be creative. It does not follow that these can be achieved only through a method of discovery.

Furthermore students, according to Skinner, do not learn simply by doing. Nor do they learn simply by exercise or practice. From experience alone a student probably learns nothing. Simply being in contact with the environment does not mean he will perceive it. For learning to occur we must recognize the response, the occasion upon which the response occurs, and the consequences of the response. In order for schools to achieve their purpose, effective control of behavior must be achieved. This is accomplished through special techniques designed to arrange reinforcement contingencies, the relations between behavior on the one hand and the consequences of that behavior on the other.

For Skinner, the application of his methods to education is simple and direct. Teaching is simply the arrangement of contingencies of reinforcement under which students learn. Although students will learn in their natural environments, it is the responsibility of a teacher to *expedite* learning and to assure the acquisition of behavior which might not otherwise be learned.

Technically speaking, what is missing from the classroom, says Skinner, is positive reinforcement. Students do not learn simply when they are shown or told. In their daily lives they behave and learn because of the consequences of their acts. Children remember because they have been reinforced for recalling what they saw or heard.

For Skinner the school is concerned with imparting to the child a large number of responses. The first task is to shape the responses, but the principal task is to bring behavior under many sorts of stimulus control. What reinforcements are involved? How soon do they follow the response? How carefully sequenced are the materials and is each step reinforced? How frequently are reinforcements provided?

First of all, Skinner asks, what reinforcements are available for teachers? The material to be learned can itself have considerable automatic reinforcement. Knowing this, most teachers plan ways to make school work more interesting. Furthermore, there are many things in a classroom that have appeal for students, such as toys, paints, scissors and paper, puzzles, library books, musical recordings. Often these sustain activity and may be used effectively by teachers as reinforcers for appropriate behavior. The net amount of reinforcement, Skinner points out, is of little significance. Very slight reinforcement can be very effective if appropriately used.

If natural reinforcers inherent in the subject matter or in the school are not enough, contrived reinforcers must be used to control behavior. For some students the secondary reinforcements found in the school are not a part of their reinforcement history and prove ineffectual. Permitting the child to engage in activities which he selects may be made contingent upon consequences of behavior to be established, such as the teacher's assignments. The approval or affection of the teacher is available as a reinforcer and is traditionally used to achieve and maintain control.

Another question is how are reinforcements to be made contingent on the appropriate behavior? Skinner's answer is that becoming competent in any subject matter area is accomplished by dividing the material into very small steps. Reinforcement must be contingent upon the completion of each step satisfactorily. By making each successive step in the schedule as small as possible, reinforcements will occur frequently.

In the traditional classroom the contingencies of reinforcement which are most efficient in controlling the student are probably beyond the capacities of a teacher. Therefore, Skinner maintains, mechanical and electrical devices must be used for most acquisition.

The Teaching Machine

The most familiar educational application of Skinner's work is undoubtedly programed instruction and teaching machines. In education the behavior to be shaped and maintained is usually verbal and it is to be brought under the control of both verbal and nonverbal stimuli. This is best accomplished by a machine.

Several kinds of teaching machines are available. Although they vary considerably in cost and complexity, most machines perform a similar function. Typically the machine provides a slot through which a statement and/or question appears. There is a second opening through which the student writes in his response or answer, usually on a separate tape. There is also some arrangement whereby the learner can move a slide to uncover the correct answer. In some machines this is done automatically when the student advances the paper to the next frame. The same movement covers his own written response with a glass slide. In this way he can compare his response with the correct one, but he cannot alter what he has written. He can then move the next statement and question into view. The machine is so arranged that one question must be completed before the next question can be seen.

Skinner believes that teaching machines have several important advantages over other methods. Students must compose their own response rather than select it from a set of alternatives. They are required to recall rather than recognize — to make responses as well as see that they are correct. In acquiring the behavior which has been programed, the student passes through a carefully designed sequence of steps, sometimes of considerable length. Each step must be so small that success is achieved, and at the same time with the step the student moves somewhat closer to the desired behavior. The machine assures that these steps are taken in a carefully prescribed order.

Although the machine itself does not teach, of course, it does bring students into contact with the teacher or person who wrote the program. In many respects, says Skinner, it is like a private tutor, in that there is a constant interchange between the program and the student. The machine keeps the student active and alert. It insists that a given point or step be mastered before the student is allowed to move on. Like a good tutor, the machine only presents material for which the student is ready. Furthermore, it helps the student to get the correct answer through the orderly construction of the program and by certain hints or prompts built into each frame of the program. And last, the machine, like a tutor, reinforces the student for every correct response by using immediate feedback to shape and maintain the behavior. The student does not need to wait for the teacher to correct papers or tell him he is right or wrong.

Clearly among the advantages of the teaching machine is that each student may progress at his own rate, completing as much work as he can in the time allowed. No one is held back by the progress of slower students nor are the slower students pressured by the performance of faster students. If a student is absent he may return and begin where he left off. By means of teaching machines, then, a teacher may supervise an entire class at the same time and yet individualize instruction. The teacher is freed from much of the mechanical and tedious classroom work, like grading papers for example. Skinner's machine lets the teacher devote his or her energies to more subtle forms of instruction, such as discussion.

Programed Materials

The success of such machines depends, naturally, on the material used in it. Many programs are commercially available today in almost any subject matter area but many teachers are learning how to write their own programs. Programs need not be used in machines; many are written in book form. A program is distinguished from a *textbook*, however, in that a book is only a source of materials to which a student exposes himself. There is no planned interaction between the book and the reader; no required responses are expected and consequently reinforcement or feedback as to the correctness of responses is not possible. Actual instruction is related to, but apart from, the text.

A program is the actual instruction, and learning is occurring during participation, not later. The student's success or failure depends on the program—not on the teacher or what happens after.

In order to illustrate a program, parts of two are presented below. The first is a set of six frames designed to teach a third- or fourth-grade pupil how to spell the word *manufacture*.[1]

1. Manufacture means to make or build. Chair factories manufacture chairs. Copy the word here:

   _ _ _ _ _ _ _ _ _ _ _
2. Part of the word is like part of the word factory. Both parts come from an old word meaning *make* or *build*.

   manu_ _ _ _ure
3. Part of the word is like part of the word manual. Both parts come from an old word for *hand*.

   _ _ _ _facture
4. The same letter goes in both spaces:

   m_nuf_cture
5. The same letter goes in both spaces:

   man_fact_re
6. Chair factories _ _ _ _ _ _ _ _ _ _ chairs.

By the time the pupil reaches frame 6 he has composed or completed the word five times. Even a poor student is likely to spell it correctly. Teaching spelling, then, is seen by Skinner as mainly a process of shaping complex forms of behavior. Programs of this sort may run to a considerable length. At five or six frames per word, spelling in grades one through four may require 20,000 to 25,000 frames, Skinner estimates. In spite of this, fifteen minutes per day on a machine should prove adequate for spelling. Thus, the machine is soon available for other students.

In the second example of programing the first eight frames of a set designed to teach about the emission of light from an incandescent source are presented.[2] In using the program, appropriate for high-school physics students, the student would write a word or phrase to complete a given item and then uncover the word shown in the column on the right.

SENTENCE TO BE COMPLETED	WORD TO BE SUPPLIED
1. The important parts of a flashlight are the battery and the bulb. When we "turn on" a flashlight, we close a switch which connects the battery with the_____.	bulb
2. When we turn on a flashlight, an electric current flows through the fine wire in the_____and causes it to grow hot.	bulb
3. When the hot wire glows brightly, we say that it gives off or sends out heat and_____.	light
4. The fine wire in the bulb is called a filament. The bulb "lights up" when the filament is heated by the passage of a(n)_____current.	electric
5. When a weak battery produces little current, the fine wire, or_____, does not get very hot.	filament
6. A filament which is less hot sends out or gives off_____ light.	less
7. "Emit" means "send out." The amount of light sent out, or "emitted," by a filament depends on how_____the filament is.	hot
8. The higher the temperature of the filament the_____ the light emitted by it.	brighter stronger

Skinner has developed a handwriting program that uses a method called *fading*. Handwriting is shaped by immediate reinforcement of the correct response and the gradual withdrawal (i.e., fading) of the controlling stimulus. The controlling stimulus might be the letter A, which the child traces. As a series of these letters are traced portions of the letter are gradually removed and the child eventually composes the entire letter himself. A special stylus and chemically treated paper are used, which change the color from black to orange when the child does not follow the letter properly. Thus immediate reinforcement is provided through this feedback as he writes and he can correct his mistakes.

A question often asked is will machines replace teachers? Certainly not, Skinner replies. They are equipment to be used to save time and labor. But the teacher's role will be changed, for many traditional practices will be affected. Consider the concept of assigning grades. If any student, given enough time, completes all that is expected in a course, he should receive an A. Comparison of the progress of one student with another serves no purpose when teaching machines are used.

How does the teaching machine embody Skinner's principles? Because the learner must emit an answer Skinner would consider the behavior to be operant in nature. Also, certain stimuli come to control the response or answer, either a question or a statement with a blank to fill in. Consequently, we have a discriminated-stimulus situation in which the emitted answers are those desired under this and only this stimulus situation. If the learner gives the correct answer, he is reinforced immediately. Reinforcement is the knowledge of results. Wrong answers presumably become extinct because they are not reinforced.

As Skinner points out, programing is still partly an art, but it is steadily moving toward a technology. "Schools and colleges have come to rely more and more on selecting students who do not need to be taught, and in doing so they have come to pay less and less attention to teaching. Among current proposals for reform, programed instruction is almost unique in focusing on the learning process and in suggesting practices which actually teach rather than select those who learn without being taught."[3]

Skinner has a great deal more to say about teaching—far more than can be treated in this book. The reader is encouraged to examine *The Technology of Teaching* for more in-depth treatment.

Strangely enough, a major concern and criticism of a technology of teaching is that a high degree of efficiency may jeopardize individuality. In a dialogue between Richard I. Evans, a professor of psychology at the University of Houston, and B. F. Skinner, Evans asked: "Do you see the possibility of controlling behavior in a manner consistent with your principles without doing violence to individuality?" Skinner replied, "Rousseau, whose book *Emile* is really a great treatise on education, was a champion of the rights of man. But at one point he slips. He says something like this: 'You will teach your student as he wants to be taught, but never forget that it is within your power to make him what you want.' And this is true. The humanist who uses persuasion, argument, inducement, emulation, or enthusiasm to get a student to learn is controlling the student just as definitely as the person who designs a program or a teaching machine."[4]

PART III

A HUMANISTIC PSYCHOLOGY: CARL R. ROGERS

There is a tradition in psychology as strong and explicit as natural scientific psychology which has attempted to define psychology as the study of the human person — the viewpoint that psychology belongs to the human sciences and not to the natural sciences.

Scientists and humanists share the same desire to understand human behavior. Their goals and their methods, however, are quite different. Psychologists who are committed to science have by and large been concerned with meeting the standards of science understood as a natural science. Encouraged by the successes of physics, chemistry, biology, and astronomy, these psychologists adopted the attitudes and methods in their study of behavior.

Because psychology conceived as a natural science has almost always been in the dominant position, those not in agreement with this approach have been seen as objectors. During the century since psychology identified itself as a science, the dissenters have voiced objections on many counts, but have never been represented as a unified group. Their weakness may be attributed in part to this fragmentation. Abraham Maslow developed the notion of the Third Force in psychology in his desire to provide a common identity for the objectors. Prominent among those psychologists who have given impetus to the Third Force movement is Carl R. Rogers.

To some within this group any science of human behavior — attempting to capture the essence of man in a set of symbolic elements and relations among these elements — is to do violence to his nature. It dehumanizes him. To these critics a scientific study of man is crude, insensitive, and superficial. By necessity science can only address

81

itself to the trivial and obvious in human behavior, thus leaving out those aspects that concern us most—his uniqueness, complexity, unpredictability.

Human scientific psychologists, such as Rogers, want a different conception of science — either a new type of science or a broader meaning of science which is faithful to the phenomena of man. To them everyday phenomena of life such as experiences, feelings, meanings, humor are psychologically relevant. In order to study them adequately, rigorously, and as they are experienced, requires conceptions, techniques, and procedures not found in the natural sciences. For Rogers, the assumptions of the natural scientific approach are not appropriate for the unique subject matter of psychology. He is willing to sacrifice precision, at least initially, in order to study the phenomena which seem to be the most relevant.

In a broad sense, most psychologists today are committed to the use of the scientific method, but there is disagreement as to the legitimate outer boundaries of this method. In the next three chapters we will examine the phenomenological viewpoint, dealing first with the historical background and philosophical assumptions followed by an account of Rogerian phenomenology and Rogers' conception of the educational process.

CHAPTER 6

Historical and Philosophical Background

The two philosophical approaches to human thought and action originally delineated in the modern world by Leibnitz and Locke, the nativistic and the empiristic, have continued to underlie many of the controversies in psychology. Those who see themselves, however, as being strictly experimentalist often disclaim any connection with so-called underlying assumptions, even going so far as did Skinner, as disavowing any interest in the task of theory formation. But to be such an experimentalist is itself an example of the direction taken by the Lockean tradition. In fact, the particular qualities of both traditions have been compounded over the years by the gradual accumulation of additional properties, which in turn have only served to distinguish further their respective adherents and to intensify their disagreements. As we have seen those attracted to the empiristic approach become analytic to the point of becoming reductionistic, objective to the point of becoming positivistic, and thus finally discarded introspection altogether as an observational technique. Those who remained in the nativistic tradition of Descartes, Leibnitz, and later Kant may be seen to have become holistically as opposed to analytically introspective and rationalistic as opposed to experimental. Although this may seem to oversimplify the history of psychology, the differentiation of the two philosophical approaches facilitates our present task in tracing the history of what is often referred to as the Third Force in psychology, that is, the humanistic approach.

In the eighteenth and early nineteenth centuries associationism in England was already encountering opposition from several sources, such as the opposition of Kant to the radically empiristic conclusions of Hume. The individual personality was thought by Hume to consist of no more than a series of experiences presented at random by the environment. If such experiences seem to define some form or

direction it is by chance of their own objective and sequential related-
ness, not by the activity of any internal, unifying agency, whether
physical or mental. But Hume also encountered opposition from his
own Scottish kinsmen, who set out to undermine the basis of association in psychology and build a new system based upon "common
sense" as opposed to strictly empiristic observation. This is not to say
that philosophers reverted to the deductive logic of scholasticism;
rather, they sought to demonstrate the unity and coherence of all
mental life through introspection. They viewed the individual as an
active entity who gives form and direction to experiences which result
from interaction with his environment.

Similar to this Scottish movement was that mentioned earlier in
Germany of faculty psychology. With its emphasis upon the "ultimate
modes of psychical functioning" it eventually made itself felt in the
formulations of Kant. In the early nineteenth century the French also
added to this continuing protest against the mechanism of the extreme empiricist view found in associationism. Under the influence of
a new era of French idealism Maine de Biran developed a truly dynamic psychology. His concern was to find the genesis of self-consciousness in the development of the child. The self was conceived
as being responsible for that individuality which is capable of observable, integrated activity. This was indeed a reaction against mechanistic approaches; the self was here being described as an experiencing
agent, rather than nothing more than a recorder capable of registering
a series of sequential experiences. De Biran believed that the self
becomes conscious of its own existence whenever a baby first begins
to make adjustments to its external environment. The very first part
of this process is primarily mechanical, crying and moving of the
limbs. But as these activities are repeated, especially whenever they
encounter resistance in the environment, a division in the field of
experience occurs. The environment is experienced as a field of objects or things upon which we react and which in turn reacts on us,
but we have in the process experienced ourselves as initiating our
own reaction. That is, we have experienced ourselves as willful
beings. To use the terms of a modern, prominent psychologist
at whom we will look later, Rollo May, we have thereby become aware
of our existence as both a subject and an object; we are both the actor
and the acted upon. To De Biran the first exercise of the will by the
human infant was the actual cause of the development of self-consciousness. This development would continue towards a greater refinement as interaction with the environment grew in complexity.
Human nature and behavior were not, then, in this system strictly

products of a dynamic interaction between a willful being capable of discriminatory action and a flexible, not altogether resistant environment.

This opposition was to British associationism and its counterpart in the developing physiological psychology in Germany and France. It was an attempt to stem the tide against reducing man's image of himself to merely another object in an orderly, lawful, but also indifferent universe. Such a mechanistic image of man had been heralded by Sir William Dampier: ". . . the whole conception of the Natural Universe has been changed by the recognition that man, subject to the same physical laws and processes as the world around him, cannot be considered separately from the world, and that scientific methods of observation, induction, deduction and experiment are applicable, not only to the original subject matter of pure science, but to nearly all the many and varied fields of human thought and activity."[1]

But earlier Blaise Pascal (1623-62), himself a colleague of Descartes in mathematics and physics, in his efforts to find a genuinely adequate means of understanding human nature, had written: "It is dangerous to show man too often that he is equal to beasts, without showing him his greatness. It is also dangerous to show him too frequently his greatness without his baseness. It is yet more dangerous to leave him ignorant of both. But, it is very desirable to show him the two together."[2]

It was in this spirit that the Scots, the German faculty psychologists, and the French idealists were all insisting on the capacity of the mind to give order to experience. In the same passage from his *Thoughts,* Pascal had also written, "Thus all our dignity lies in thought."[3] As we have seen, behaviorists, the long-term heirs to radical empiricism, did away with assumptions about internal origins. In retrospect, they would interpret these earlier, rather idealistic conceptions of a unitary substance or principle as expressions of an atavistic metaphysics. Behaviorists, as had Hume before them, view the human personality as but a transitory configuration which has been brought into being by particular environmental stimuli. Contrary to the tradition in which we saw the Frenchman Maine de Biran hypothesize the existence of an internal integrated structure termed the self, behaviorists deny any kind of material, continuing self-contained structure which may exhibit generalizing qualities over any particular environmental situation. In an attempt to find a middle ground in this continuing controversy David Ausubel wrote this rebuttal to "the more extreme of these theorists":

This view of personality is rationalized on the grounds that since an individual's behavior does in fact vary every time the situational context is altered, it must therefore be determined by the latter variable alone. It is hardly necessary to point out, however, that the demonstration of behavioral change associated with variability in one factor does not necessarily preclude the possibility that other variables are simultaneously operative. In fact, by simply reversing the picture, i.e., keeping the situation constant and varying the individuals exposed to it, one could just as easily emerge with the equally one-sided conclusion that only personality factors determine behavioral change.[4]

No doubt it has become obvious to the reader that the questions asked as to the nature of human personality are intimately tied up with the epistomological questions concerning how man is to be studied, that is, investigated and generalized about. It should be noted, perhaps, that even the choice of terms to describe the subject under investigation — human consciousness, personality, or mental structures and qualities — as opposed to specifically human behavior — presupposes a certain basic methodological orientation. The theologian Maurice Friedman in his critical analysis of several possible "contemporary images of man" surveys a wide gamut of such orientations, from Henri Bergson's "vitalism" and Aldous Huxley's "modern mysticism" to the scientism of such persons as Sigmund Freud and Erich Fromm and the "pragmatism" (an outgrowth of British empiricism) of others like William Jones, John Dewey, and Harry Stack Sullivan.[5] Unfortunately, Friedman omitted consideration of behaviorism. But the point is, relative to such a wide distribution of possible images of man, both the nativistic and empiristic positions discussed in this book should be viewed within the context of a developing scientific orientation.

Of course, the extremists in the empiricist tradition would deny this and maintain that there are only two, rather clearly defined possible orientations, their own and the metaphysical. But in comparison to such a wide range as that surveyed by Friedman neither the Scots nor the French idealists made investigations in any other manner save that of empirical observation. Such was the continuing influence of the Lockean tradition. The conflict, then, between the two approaches was already seemingly evolving toward a question of loyalty — loyalty to the subject matter under investigation as compared with loyalty to the method of investigation.

Thus, by the end of the nineteenth century it had become increasingly clear that a choice between these two traditions meant the choice between viewing psychology as a natural science, that is, a science which consistently models itself after the methodology of the natural sciences, as compared with viewing it as a human science, an approach whose methodology consists of and is derived from its primary concern with its human subject matter. And though from 1879 with the founding of Wundt's famous laboratory in Leipzig until recently the latter view has prevailed, it is fair to say that it never did go unchallenged. There were always a few dissident philosophers of science and even psychologists themselves who never ceased in their attempts to define psychology as the study of the human person.

According to H. A. Hodges, editor of an introductory work on the German philosopher Wilhelm Dilthey (1833-1911), and Amedeo Giorgi, a contemporary professor of psychology and advocate of this minority view, it was Dilthey who more succinctly than ever before, discerned the distinctive character of a human science. Hodges wrote this summarizing statement of Dilthey's orientation:

[Dilthey] points to the dominating position which has been held, in most periods of philosophical history, by the study of the problems presented by mathematics and the natural sciences. . . . But, says Dilthey, we are now in a position to see that it constitutes only one half of the globus intellectualis; the other half is composed of the study of man in society and in history. Here we meet with a different type of study. Instead of observing our object directly, we have to approach it indirectly through written testimony and other similar evidence; instead of clearly formulated theories which can be tested by experiment, we have an attempt to analyze and describe the concrete complexities of life; instead of explanation of particular events and processes through general laws, we have an appreciative understanding of the meaning and value of the unique individual. There is no reason why the one sphere of knowledge should not be as thoroughly studied by philosophers as the other.[6]

In criticizing the natural scientific approach to psychology, Dilthey was clearly not suggesting that it should become metaphysical or even art. He pointed instead to a position between the natural sciences and art as the rightful orientation of this disciplined study. He believed that the human sciences necessarily must deal with the human world of meaning and value, those products of an active mind and a free will. Experience must be studied and interpreted as that phenomena which express inner, spiritual reality. Such phenomena, unlike the data with which the natural sciences are concerned, cannot be removed from their historical context, as it is within this context that human activity occurs, that action is taken and consequences incurred by free willed, conscious, and necessarily responsible beings. It cannot be the purpose of such an orientation to formulate laws, but rather to discern and formulate systems of value. Even Skinner raised, albeit factitiously, the question, how can one have a science about a creature which hops about capriciously?

For Dilthey, psychology as a natural science was often instructive when it talked about sensations and their attributes. But it really made no genuine contribution in the realm of those phenomena which constituted the definitive core of being human. That is, it had nothing to say in respect to creative imagination, self-consciousness, self-sacrifice, and a sense of obligation, love, devotion, and sympathy. Actually, Dilthey saw the other end of the spectrum, metaphysical speculation, the arts, literature, as having had, heretofore, much more to offer in regard to such categories. He desired not, however, that psychology should seek a model from this direction, but that it take the wisdom and insights of the poets and give them precise expression and a rigorous, systematic grounding.

Perhaps Dilthey's most scathing indictment of that view of psychology as a natural science was in the distinction he drew between the "descriptive" sciences and the "explanatory" sciences.[7] He agreed that all the sciences must seek to determine laws which express the interrelatedness of the data under observation. But he argued that a descriptive science is one whose laws are found by true empirical analysis, that is, by close examination of what is given in experience. An explanatory science on the other hand is one which takes its laws from a methodological assumption which determines their general nature beforehand. Such an assumption, according to Dilthey, is no more than a mere hypothetical construction. In other words, Dilthey supported the claim that psychology as a human science is, in fact, the consistently true heir to the empiricist tradition, since it takes as data that which is actually given in the individual experience of consciousness. This is clearly a definitive statement as to what is called a "phenomenologically" based approach. He even appears to have drawn a close parallel between what amounts to medieval scholasticism (truth being based upon preconceived notions and assumptions) and its traditional opposite, the natural sciences.

Carl Rogers, a recognized leader of contemporary humanistic psychology and an outspoken critic of the Skinnerian approach, has himself most recently done the same. Included in his remarks at a conference called to examine "some of the very specific problems which plague the behavioral scentist" were the following:

Are we willing for the model and the methods of our science to emerge naturally from the problems of our science? Can we work at the central issues—whether a question of brain function, memory storage, response to love, the influence of the group on attitudes, the significances of values in behavior, or whatever—and simply evolve methods pertinent and relevant to those issues? Can we build a psychological science, or a behavioral science which grows out of the problems encountered in the study of the whole man in his subjective and objective being? Or must we feel that our science can only be a copy of Newtonian science—a model already out-dated in its own field?[8]

The views of Dilthey in these remarks are clearly suggestive of the direction to be taken by the human sciences.

If Dilthey's advocation of a humanistically based approach was somewhat ignored by his contemporaries, however, such was not the case with Franz Brentano (1838-1917). Brentano's advocations directly influenced an experimental trend first known as the Wurzburg School, which opposed Wundt's structuralism and later was succeeded by two contemporary psychological systems, Gestalt and Field Theory. This is not to say that Brentano was insisting on psychology becoming a strictly experimental science. In fact, though respecting the results of such experimentation, he held that an overemphasis in that direction might well mean elevating a concern for method over the primary issue of human consciousness. Furthermore, like Dilthey, but very much unlike Wundt, Brentano held that psychology can be an empirical human science without following the dictates of the experimental, natural sciences.

Brentano's famous work, *Psychology from an Empirical Standpoint*, was published in the same year, 1874, that the more orthodox experimental psychologist, Wundt, also published his first handbook on physiological psychology. Brentano was convinced that neither the associationist tradition in Great Britain nor the experimental physiology school of Germany was on the right track. Both of these approaches had been developing an analytical method that reduces consciousness to elements—sensations, images, and feelings. Brentano argued that consciousness consists of conscious functions, that is, acts or phenomena, not of mere sensations. He insisted that the particular manifestations of consciousness, which he called psychic phenomena, are the ultimate data of psychological studies. He considered such phenomena to be irreducible and characterized by their intentionality.

Herein lay the key to Brentano's view of psychology as a human science—intentionality, willfulness, purpose. His psychology was the study of conscious processes in which the "act" rather than the content of experience was central. This view entails a distinction between experience as an objective structure and experience as a way of acting. In the case of seeing red, the true subject matter of psychology is not the particular sensation of red, but the process of experiencing red. The emphasis is on the mind as an active agent in such a process in that it pointed to something outside of itself, as opposed to whatever particular objective qualities with which an object may be endowed (redness in this case).

Before leaving the nineteenth century, mention should be made of that American psychologist who is today claimed as a forerunner by both behaviorism and humanistic psychology, William James. Giorgi points out that James never achieved a unified viewpoint precisely because he was torn between meeting the demands for a system of psychology of the natural sciences and yet refusing to abandon the investigation of those kinds of phenomena—stream of consciousness, will, experience—relevant to psychology as a human science. Having ing been too influenced by his times, according to Giorgi, James conceded that psychology was only "the hope of a science." In the following, his refusal to accept a mechanistic view of human behavior is apparent:

> The pursuance of future ends and the choice of means for their attainment are thus the mark and criterion of the presence of mentality in a phenomenon. We all use this test to discriminate between an intelligent and a mechanical performance. We impute no mentality to sticks and stones, because they never seem to move for the sake of anything, but always when pushed, and then indifferently and with no sign of choice.[9]

We have, thus far, examined the continuing controversy between philosophers oriented towards one or the other of the two traditions going back to Locke and Leibnitz. With the official birth of psychology as a science in the latter half of the nineteenth century, the controversy became transmuted. The debate became centered on questions as to how scientific the new discipline was to be or, rather, as to what kind of science orientation should it have—naturalistic or humanistic. In the twentieth century we want to look at two rather significant influences that have reinforced the view of psychology as a human science. One of these claims the status of being somewhat empirical, often quantitative, and even experimental. The other is grounded on a view or image of man that is derived from one of the century's most prominent philosophical systems.

If Wundtian analytical introspection was finally viewed as inadequate, especially in America, by those responding to Watson's call for a science of behavior, it was also seen in Germany as artificial when applied to a description of perception. Perception may be defined as an event within the person, perhaps initiated by the excitation of sensory receptors, yet also significantly influenced by other factors of a kind that can be shown to have originated in the life history of the person. Perception seemed to have characteristics that could not be adequately reduced to sensations and their attributes as delineated by Wundt. Influenced by Brentano and perhaps by Dilthey, several dissenters developed what has sometimes been called an "experimental" phenomenology, that is, "Gestalt" psychology or a psychology of form. Eventually this movement was brought to America and prior to the Second World War constituted the main opposition to behaviorism.

A basic premise of Gestalt theory is that the manner in which any particular object is perceived is a function of the total configuration or field in which the object is set. Furthermore, such a perceptual field is composed of more than just its specific parts, that is, specific objects; rather, it is also composed of relationships, discerned by the observing individual to be in existence between such parts or field components. Thus, it is the perception of relationships that make up the experience of an individual at any given moment. This, of course, is a modern restatement of that ancient, pre-Socratic principle which denies the possibility of explaining wholes by a study of their constituent parts. The Platonists themselves sought to demonstrate through mathematical formulations general laws of arrangement, synthesis, and order. But it was the Gestaltist Max Wertheimer who demonstrated in 1912 a piece of experience, movement, that could not be explained by reduction to any objective attributes. Light was thrown through a small slit arranged vertically. A moment later light was thrown through a second slit inclined some degrees to the right. No actual movement of light was involved. Yet light was perceived by the viewing subject as having "fallen" from one position to another. In the experience of the observer, movement had apparently taken place. This experience was obviously interdependent with what had occurred in the "objective world" but was not, nevertheless, determined by it. Rather, it was the perception of a recognizable or meaningful relationship between the sensations of light that determined the nature of the experience as it was actually experienced.

Wertheimer was in protest against the general modern scientific movement from parts to whole, from elements to structures, from below to above. He insisted that the attributes of any discernible system, insofar as they can be defined, are defined by their relation to the system as a whole in which they are functioning. Furthermore, he also maintained that there are general directions in which the emergence of structured wholes are predictable. That is, if an unstable structure is given, in which certain types of inner relationships are perceived, one can predict what kind of organization must eventually supervene — one that is most orderly, balanced, and comprehensive, or as Wertheimer preferred, one which has *Pragnanz*. Pragnanz is the quality of self-fulfillment which is intrinsic in all structured totals. This includes the cognitive and affective capacities of living systems as well.

It is important to emphasize that Gestaltists did not conceive of the perceiver as actually creating order, but rather as apprehending it as being objectively there in the world. But on the other hand, there never is perceived the totality of the objective world. This means that perception is a process experienced relative to an objective reality. Involved in the movement of perception from that which is incomplete toward that which is more nearly complete is a continuous dynamic selection and integration of forms (Gestaltan). Thus an explanation of such experience must entail not only an apprehension of the order existing in the world but also of that internal order which the perceiver manifests as he passes from one new integration to another.

A younger colleague of Wertheimer, Wolfgang Kohler, sought to demonstrate as incorrect the Thorndike hypothesis that learning depends simply upon trial and error and upon the stamping-in of the correct responses. In various experiments with apes he concluded that solutions to problems are found by a process of integration or insight, in which not a number of separate elements of the problem taken in series, but an integrated system of elements or clues, is responded to all at once. Learning was held to entail the progressive realization of forms rather than the accretion of or response to separate elements of a problem.

According to Gardner Murphy, a historian of modern psychology, the general tendency in America was to regard Gestalt psychology as providing interesting insights and a direction for further research. That is, it was not regarded as it was in Germany as a final or complete, all-embracing theoretical formulation. Nevertheless, mention should be made of one of its offshoots which did attain that status — Field Theory as formulated by Kurt Lewin. On the one hand, it may seem odd to include in our historical tracing of humanistic psychology even this short mention of Lewin's Theory, for its whole method of representing psychological reality was borrowed directly from the latest viewpoints of the physical sciences (electromagnetic field concept of physics). However, Dilthey and Brentano had both urged that psychology as a human science be willing to consider data derived by a number of methods but be dominated by none.

Lewin himself had been a physicist before he joined the Gestalt movement. But even his earliest research on the dynamics of memory had been aimed at refuting the behaviorist orientation. Thorndike himself later agreed that Lewin was correct in asserting that a sheer successive presentation of stimuli produced no actual functional connections between them. And, though greater detail is beyond the scope of the present work, suffice it to point out those principal characteristics of Lewin's field theory that lend themselves in support of psychology as a human science: (1) A field is considered to be the totality of coexisting facts—external and internal—which are conceived of as mutually interdependent. (2) Behavior is a function of this field or *life space* which exists at the moment behavior occurs (like Rogerian phenomenology, and unlike Freudian psychoanalytic theory, Lewin's theory is ahistorical). (3) Analysis begins with the situation as a whole (experience as it is given). The word "phenomenal" may be defined as that which is perceived in contrast with that which is real. But, as we have noted with Gestalt Theory, this does not mean that what is perceived is necessarily something other than that which is real. We shall see later, in fact, that Carl Rogers tends to define mental health as the congruence of the two. What it does mean in terms of a psychological science is that what is significant in order to explain a given behavior is that which is perceived or experienced as orderly and meaningful at any given moment as opposed to any objective reality. Behavior is determined, therefore, by the inner experience of the organism as it gives order and value to its environment. A science of behavior must necessarily have, then, a phenomenologically based approach. It must be a science of the person.

Rollo May, a contemporary of Rogers in the humanist movement, in his book, *Psychology and the Human Dilemma*, attempts to support the orientation of a science of man by choosing as a basis for psychotherapy that image of man derived from existentialist philosophy. He makes no apology to the behaviorists for what they would consider to be a merely philosophical as opposed to a rigorously scientific approach. In fact, like Dilthey he characterizes behavioral scientists as being oftentimes completely unaware that this very process of looking objectively at the facts is itself based on particular philosophical assumptions. May also considers it by no means absurd to suggest a close relation between our (American) inherited, moralistic, frontiersmen's puritanism and a preoccupation with behavior in our study of man. In addition simply to the admonition to children to "behave! behave! behave!" there is also perhaps a threat to the traditional self-reliance of Americans inherent in any predisposition to subjectivity and introspection. But threat or no threat, May maintains that we can never have a science of man without considering such subjective categories as man's inner being, its expression in action, and the meaning derived from action. In answer to those who would denounce such considerations as a return to metaphysical speculation, May quotes Michael Polanyi, professor emeritus in chemistry, medicine, and social studies, Oxford University. Polanyi, who writes that his main professional concern is "to establish a better foundation than we now possess for holding the beliefs by which we live and must live, though unable adequately to justify them today,"[10] also wrote this warning concerning modern science: "In the days when an idea could be silenced by showing that it was contrary to religion, theology was the greatest single source of fallacies. Today, when any human thought can be discredited by branding it as unscientific, the power previously exercised by theology has passed over to science; hence science has become in its turn the greatest single source of error."[11]

Hazel Barnes writes in her introduction to her translation of Jean-Paul Sartre, "To my mind this aspect of Sartre's existentialism is one of his most positive and most important contributions — the attempt to make contemporary man look for himself again and refuse to be absorbed in a role on the stage of a puppet theater."[12] It is now generally recognized that existentialism, characterized by Maurice Friedman as "a mood embracing a number of disparate philosophies," is as old as Pascal, a colleague of Descartes.[13] In fact, Friedman sees Sartre as ". . . . a sort of latter-day Cartesian dualist who, if he does not make a strict division between mind and body, nonetheless holds consciousness to be free only when it transcends itself through its own becoming, . . . but bound when it must see itself as an object seen by others, as attached to the body, as conditioned and imprisoned within its own incarnation."[14]

But Sartre is also somewhat recognized in this century as having crystalized this mood into a specific image of man, as that sole being which invents himself and has no meaning or value prior to his doing so. Even to exist as a body bound and imprisoned is a situation so chosen. This is what Sartre means when he defines existentialism as existence preceding essence. For Sartre, man is a being of whom no essence can be finally affirmed, for such an essence would imply a permanent structure, contradictory to man's power of transforming himself indefinitely. In Sartre is found, therefore, what is perhaps the most radical affirmation of human freedom and potentiality ever made.

In *Existential Psychoanalysis,* Sartre criticizes modern psychology in general as being altogether too deterministic. He maintains that man cannot be understood at all if we see in him only what our study of animal life permits us to see, or if we reduce him to naturalistic or mechanical determinisms. This is also the case if we reduce and separate him into instincts or sets of stimuli and responses, or in any other way consider the subject of our study apart from what constitutes his humanness—his ultimate freedom and responsibility. Mention of some of the more central points developed by Sartre in this book is intended to show the significance of his influence and contribution to a humanistically based approach in psychology.

First, Sartre, like Dilthey and other phenomenological psychologists, insists on understanding and describing as opposed to explaining. Explanations estrange the observer from the person observed. They represent an attempt to apply a general, abstract law to a unique, particular person. In fact, explanations cannot even do what they are intended to do. For instance, those having to do with environmental determinants do not succeed as explanations because they fail to account for that moment of decision which must ensue whenever a man, acting as subject, chooses for, against, or among such influences. An individual is influenced by the environment only as he transforms that influence into a concrete situation having value and meaning for himself. This coincides with that view of Rollo May's which sees human freedom as derived, not from man's capacity to live as pure subject, but rather in the capacity to experience himself as in a dialectical oscillation between two poles of a dilemma, as both subject and object.

Second, Sartre sees human existence as purposive. Human reality identifies and defines itself by the ends which it pursues, not by hypothetical causes in the past. Neither is it possible to live without purpose—to live simply to live. Even such a life entails the continual choosing of same. (It is interesting to point out that Sartre views Western bourgeois society as decadent and meaningless. But he is, in doing so, inconsistent. To fight so vehemently against such a society presupposes a conflict of purposes and values by each party. To be anti-Christ presupposes Christ.)

Similarly, Sartre insists that such purpose and meaning is derived not from any universal reality, as French and German idealists have postulated, but rather from the concrete, particular realities of those situations called into existence by individual choice. The way of man is unique for each particular man because each man is unique and each is in a unique situation. This is what the nineteenth-century German existentialist, Fredrich Nietzsche, was expressing in this dialogue from *Thus Spake Zarathustra:* "This—is now my way—where is yours?" says Zarathustra. "Thus did I answer those who asked me 'the way.' For 'the' way—it doth not exist!" Martin Heidegger, a contemporary German existentialist, also interprets Nietzsche's famous proclamation, "God is dead!" in precisely these terms.[15] It portrays, according to Heidegger, the existentialist's denial of any world of ideal essences and their insistence on the world of the here and now.

Finally, we should specifically emphasize the concept of ontology—the study of being and becoming. Sartre would have the central concern of psychology to be the rediscovery, through an examination of present, concrete situations, of the original mode of existence in which an individual had chosen his being. The subjective choice by which each person makes himself a person must be brought to light in a strictly objective form. Sartre agrees with the phenomenological position of the Gestaltists concerning wholes and their parts. He argues that the whole can be understood by examining that moment when a person chooses and commits himself as a totality in a concrete relationship with the world. His most famous statement, "I am my choices," sums up what he means by this totality—an essence which entails both freedom and responsibility, both actuality and potentiality.

The significance, then, of existentialism to a science of man lies in its particular restatement and emphasis of that tradition which goes back to Descartes, the view of human thought and behavior as having essentially an internal origin. In a symposium on existential psychology, Abraham Maslow had rhetorically asked: "What's in European existentialism for the American psychologist?" In summing up Maslow's own answer to that question, Gordon Allport, his colleague in the humanistic psychology movement, stated: "Existentialism deepens the concerns that define the human condition. In so doing, it prepares the way for the first time for a psychology of mankind."[16]

Maslow and Allport, along with Rollo May, have written extensively on existential psychology. They have been designated by Rogers along with himself as that core group of contemporary American psychologists which constitutes a humanistically based opposition to behaviorism. According to Rogers these "voices" are saying that: "the tunnel vision of behavior is not adequate to the whole range of human phenomena," and that ". . . human behavior is in some significant ways, something more than the behavior of our laboratory animals."[17] Rogers himself has been looked to by these, his colleagues, as having suggested viable means by which existential dogma may be recast into testable propositions. These men have not turned aside from empirical research, rather they only desire a science which considers the whole person and which elevates this prerequisite over any particular concern for method.

Thus our historical survey is ended. We will consider now the contemporary status of this "third force" movement in psychology as it is defined by Carl Rogers, the man described by his cohort, Rollo May, as being one of the two psychologists "who are widely known as the representatives of the two horns of this dilemma," the human dilemma, man as subject or man as object, B. F. Skinner, of course, being the other representative.[18]

CHAPTER 7

The Process of Learning:
Roger's Phenomenology

It was pointed out earlier that Rogers has devoted most of his professional life to clinical work in an endeavor to understand and be of therapeutic help to specific individuals. This background as a clinical psychologist is in contrast to most of the persons whose work has been thus far considered in this book. Rogers has been working with people in clinical situations as opposed to working with animals in laboratories. Neither has he been primarily or simply academic, that is, concerned only with speculation apart from real-life situations. To point this out is not to be merely pedantic. In fact, we shall see that it constitutes his major claim to verifiability. For it is from this clinical experience that Rogers has developed his various theoretical positions in regard to several areas of concern in psychology and even in education.

We will turn now to an examination of his theoretical formulation in several areas: scientific methodology, psychological counseling or therapy, personality, interpersonal relationships, mental health, and learning. In so doing his identification with and contributions to a humanistically based approach to psychology will become manifest as being both historically significant as well as somewhat contemporarily definitive.

In *Client-Centered Therapy* (1951) Rogers presented 19 formal principles regarding human behavior. All are concerned with learning from a phenomenological viewpoint: (1) the development of an individual's own sense of reality, (2) those internal forces which cause him to act, and (3) the development of the individual's own self-concept, that is, his concept of himself as a person who acts. Inherent in all 19 principles is Rogers' assumption of man's ability to adapt, that is, his propensity to grow in a direction that enhances his existence. Such positive growth may, however, be stunted or mistakenly directed, if the individual's unique sense or picture of reality is not congruent with reality. In this regard we shall examine one of Rogers' primary contributions: that given a non-threatening environment in which an individual may experiment with the various possible modes of being available to him, congruence with reality will increase and positive growth again resume. This section, then, will be centered on 19 principles of Rogerian phenomenology.

1. Every individual exists in a continually changing world of experience of which he is the center.

An individual is in the world and he, so to speak, has a world. The latter is continually changing. The meaning of this statement is very similar to that encountered in our discussion of Gestalt psychology and Field theory. A person, for instance, is engaged in an activity. Sense receptors are being stimulated which altogether provide a larger world of experience—the phenomenal field—than that necessary for the activity. Some of this experience is therefore ignored, although generally available to awareness. The phenomenal field is constituted by the figure (that which is immediately given in consciousness) and the ground (that which is ignored). If the specific activity is perceived as boring or irrelevant, the entire field may be altered as something in the ground is made prominent instead. Thus the phenomenal world changes according to the internal states of the individual.

Being the center of such a world means, of course, that this world of experience, though often including others, is fundamentally private. Only the individual who has a world can have that world available to his consciousness, can know his experiences as they are immediately given in their totality. Communication between individuals is, therefore, not only difficult but necessarily incomplete, and often inadequate or distorted. In fact, it occurs only as the individual at the center of his world perceives any bit of new experience to be similar or relevant to his previous experience. You may try to convey to me the thrill of skiing as you have experienced it. My understanding of your experience will be greatly facilitated, if I can bring into awareness my own previous experiences with mountains or speed or snow and thus have some idea of what you are saying or what you have experienced and what that experience has meant to you. But my understanding of what you have experienced will necessarily be incomplete. Phenomenologically, we exist in our worlds as islands unto ourselves.

*2. The organism reacts to the field as it is experienced and per-
ceived. This perceptual field is, for the individual, his "reality."*

Umpires at baseball games are often thought of as "blind" by
those home town fans who have, supposedly, more reliable vision.
Our enemies in war are, of course, cruel and demonic while to us "war
is hell." The child who hides a comic book behind his history text
evidently perceives the events imagined by one author to be more
relevant to his world than those imagined by another. We have all
experienced judging someone's behavior as being, perhaps, "stupid"
or "irrational" and yet later having altered this judgment as extenuat-
ing circumstances come to light. It might be more correct to say that
such circumstances have been brought into our own awareness. For
apparently, they already existed as "light" for the person so judged.
"Reality" is, therefore, a given, unique experience in an individual's
phenomenal world. His behavior will reflect not, perhaps, our perception of reality, but necessarily his own. Behavior depends upon
the subjective reality of the phenomenal field, not upon the stimulat-
ing conditions of any external, environmental reality.

If the above, then, is indeed the case, the question might be asked:
how can we know what is "really" real? Defined phenomenologically,
"reality" becomes purely a hypothetical concept which accounts for
the totality of all conditions imposed by the external world upon an
individual. But since other individuals are included in each of our
fields of experience, it does become possible as we make identification of similarly perceived phenomenon to form consensus groups. In
fact, we often tend to ignore and even push out of awareness those
persons and their assumptions regarding what is real which do not
correspond to our own. However, such a lack of consensus also af-
fords us the opportunity of checking our hypothesis about reality. We
may change our concepts about reality and thus in doing so facilitate
changes in our phenomenal world of experience. Scientists, for instance, deliberately set out to get a consensus of both their procedures and their conclusions. If they are successful in this quest, their
conclusions are considered by the consensus group as constituting an
addition to a factual body of sharable knowledge. This process is
somewhat in contrast, for example, to those religious experiences
considered to be mystical. By their nature they are not always available for communication to others. However, even the scientific re-
searcher must finally evaluate the consequences of his research in
his own, personal phenomenological field. To use a cliché: truth as
beauty exists in eyes of the beholder.

3. *The organism reacts as an organized whole to this phenomenal field.*

All aspects of an individual's being—both physical and mental or emotional—enter into behavior as interdependent elements in the world of experience. A reaction to having a hand burned by a hot stove might include the immediate response of withdrawal of same, but it also might include application of medication, an explanation to another of what occurred, or even loss of appetite. Thought processes are thought often to interfere with normal or automatic body processes. People have been known to have had physical discomfort allayed by their belief that a certain medication, considered by their doctor to be incapable of producing any effect, would do the trick. This principle, then, is essentially holistic. In the area of learning, it supports the idea of learning by insight. A person learns a task through perception of the relationships that exist in his phenomenal field.

4. *The organism has one basic tendency and striving: to actualize, maintain, and enhance the experiencing organism.*

The reader may well recognize this principle as dealing with motivation, a concept for which innumerable drives or energy systems, needs, motives, or environmental determiners have been suggested. But Rogers accounts for all of these in this one basic assumption, corresponding it would seem, with the basic idea of survival in evolutionary theory. The organism is considered to be a purely monistic dynamic system; one drive suffices to account for all behavior. There is here no mind-body duality. However, by actualizing, the organism experiences increased differentiation within the phenomenal field. With a baby this may be simply the first sense of differentiation from the mother. The other extreme might be thought of as that sense of uniqueness experienced in the creative arts. Self-actualization is thus characterized by all kinds of behavior, both physical and cognitive. But in all cases the basis for behavior is the individual's own perception of that which is necessary for such actualization.

Distorted perception may lead, however, to destruction rather than self-actualization. Later, we will see how this might occur. Suffice it now to point out that given the opportunity, that is, if opportunity for enhancement rather than contraction of the phenomenal field is perceived, a forward tendency will normally result. Those phenomena related to such enhancement will tend to dominate the field of experience. There is, then, in this principle a basis for an ethical system based upon the idea that man is inherently "good."

Behaviorists, of course, see man as essentially neutral. But the standards of this "goodness" would still be difficult to establish. They cannot be generalized as absolute for all men at all times. For they can only be realized in the self-actualizing processes of each individual. In fact, only retardation of the process could result from any such generalization made operable by environmental manipulators (all those agents of socialization such as teachers, preachers, or even parents).

5. *Behavior is basically the goal-directed attempt of the organism to satisfy its need as experienced in the perceived field.*

All behavior is, thus, viewed as purposive. Purpose derives from phenomenon being perceived as obstacle, to self-actualization and enhancement. Hunger may be such an obstacle; so might a highly directive authority figure. The external environment may provide the obstacle; however, it does not, thereby, specifically determine the goal-orientation or purpose which is eventually expressed in behavior. The individual's phenomenal field may undergo a series of ground to figure changes, thus providing several possible alternatives to respond to. To the observer the resulting behavior may seem irrelevant, inadequate, or even destructive. But in any case his judgment cannot have been based on all available evidence. Such evidence or reasons for a course of action are only available to perception within the behaver's own field of experience.

6. *Emotion accompanies and in general facilitates such goal-directed behavior, the kind of emotion being related to the seeking versus the consummatory aspects of the behavior, and the intensity of the emotion being related to the perceived significance of the behavior for the maintenance and enhancement of the organism.*

This is not a statement regarding causality. The cause of behavior is not necessarily physiological changes which the body undergoes, though these may enter into the phenomenal field and be responded to by the individual. For example, a nervous speaker realizes that his mouth is dry and takes a drink to relieve this uncomfortable state. These emotions exist as part of the total reaction of the individual to his phenomenal field. Such behavior is purposive, that is, goal-directed; emotions must necessarily lend themselves to the perceived purposes of the organism. These kinds of emotions are those that aid in preparing the individual for action—fear, excitement or joy, or general unpleasantness—as opposed to those experienced in the aftermath of completed behavior—feelings of satisfaction, relaxation, calmness.

To the observer of another individual's behavior, it would seem that often these accompanying emotions may retard rather than facilitate goal-directed behavior. For instance, a student may get so excited over an impending exam that he may "freeze up" at the crucial time. But this too-intense emotional reaction is not really due to the exam; it accompanies instead the meaning ascribed within the phenomenal field to one part of that field, the exam and its consequences as perceived by the individual relative to maintenance and enhancement needs. The problem in behavior may well lie in a distortion of reality, that is, in the meaning so ascribed within the field of experience to the impending exam. Such an ascription of meaning might occur due to the individual's perceiving his phenomenal field as overwhelmingly threatening to his existence at the moment.

7. *The best vantage point for understanding behavior is from the internal frame of reference of the individual himself.*

This principle reemphasizes the uniqueness of each individual's world of being. German phenomenologists would say "being there" in the world. Caution must be exercised in any evaluation of another's behavior, since any such evaluation must necessarily be from an external vantage point. But another's behavior may be somewhat understood empathically. Otherwise, communication would be impossible. This is not just being sympathetic in the sense of having pity or showing tolerance, though it may often result in both of these behaviors by the observing individual. Prejudice would be significantly diminished if empathy becomes the conscious and purposeful mode of communication. It means, rather, genuinely trying to identify in your own phenomenal field those elements and relationships which may appear to reproduce for you those field conditions being experienced by the individual whose behavior you are observing. Obviously, such attempts will necessarily and always be only partially successful.

8. *A portion of the total perceptual field gradually becomes differentiated as the "self."*

Rogers primarily emphasizes processes of change and development, rather than particular structural constructs. This is in keeping with his phenomenologically based approach. However, there are two structural constructs which are of fundamental importance to this theory: *the organism* and *the self.* His entire theory has often been labeled as "self-theory." He has described how he came to adopt this concept:

Speaking personally, I began my work with the settled notion that the "self" was a vague, ambiguous, scientifically meaningless term which had gone out of the psychologist's vocabulary with the departure of the introspectionists. Consequently I was slow in recognizing that when clients were given the opportunity to express their problems and their attitudes in their own terms, without any guidance or interpretation, they tended to talk in terms of the self. . . . It seemed clear . . . that the self was an important element in the experience of the client, and that in some odd sense his goal was to become his "real self."[1]

The totality of all which is potentially available to awareness, that is, experience, constitutes the phenomenal field of the living organism. A portion of this field becomes differentiated as a self. This is that part of the phenomenal field which is aware of being and functioning in the world, which knows that it exists, which knows that it is an organism and that it has experiences. This is not to say that it is always present to awareness, but that it is always available, for it is the being that actually has the experience of such awareness. Rogers wrote that the self-concept denotes "the organized, consistent conceptual gestalt composed of perceptions of the characteristics of the 'I' or 'me' and the perceptions of the relationships of the 'I' or 'me' to others and to various aspects of life, together with the values attached to these perceptions. It is a gestalt which is available to awareness though not necessarily in awareness. It is a fluid and changing gestalt, a process, but at any given moment it is a specific entity."[2]

9. *As a result of interaction with the environment and, particularly, as a result of evaluational interaction with others, the structure of self is formed — an organized, fluid, but consistent conceptual pattern of perceptions of characteristics and relationships of the "I" or "me" together with values attached to these concepts.*

The means by which the process of differentiation occurs is very near that proposed by the Frenchman, Maine de Biran. The very important addition, reflecting the influence of existential phenomenology, is that of all parts of the phenomenal field, that which is differentiated as self is defined as having particular meaning or value. An infant may experience as exciting the moving of his head back and forth. If he should bump his head on the crib, he experiences a sense of division and a process of evaluation in his phenomenal field. But he finds the additional element, bumping his head, less meaningful to his enhancement than simply moving his head. Apparently, consistent patterns of relationships form within the phenomenal field regarding "me" and "not me" as well as evaluations of possible actions as being either desirable or undesirable, good or bad. Some more specifically interrelated parts of the field become more valuable or necessary for purposes of enhancement—such as reactions of delight by parents to the behavior of a "good" baby. These parts are thus eventually incorporated into that phenomenal structure within the field which is characterized as having more permanency and internal consistency, that is, the self-structure. In the case of the relationship between the perceived delight of the parents and the particular behavior of the "me," the "me" becomes perceived as "good." The reverse may also occur, of course, as is apparent with rejected children, that is, those negatively evaluated by their parents.

10. The values attached to experiences, and the values which are a part of the self-structure, in some instances are values experienced directly by the organism, and in some instances are values introjected or taken over from others, but perceived in distorted fashion as if they had been experienced directly.

The process of differentiation and evaluation resulting from the child's moving and then bumping his head is an example derived from direct experience. Eating candy, playing games, or perhaps reading an interesting book are perceived as good and are direct experiences. But many potential experiences are evaluated indirectly. They are considered as good or bad on the basis of interaction with people who have been previously evaluated as particularly important to the existing self-structure. Psychological maladjustment may result if a large number of introjected values become closely related with the self-structure and conflict with direct experience.

To illustrate, consider a common, but nevertheless complex, example of introjected values which have had much to do with defining sex roles in our society. A young girl experiences herself as being loved and lovable on the basis of years in which interaction has been primarily with her parents. Affection has often been communicated by the parents with gifts such as dolls, nursing games, or party dresses perceived by the child as fun to play with. But they also produce in the phenomenal field an image of appropriate behavior, likely to maintain and enhance the "lovable" self-structure. As peer contacts increase and perhaps as the child discovers such typical outdoor adventures as climbing trees or running barefoot, conflict with parents might occur over what behavior to choose for self-enhancement. Statements that suggest that an activity is "not for young ladies" or is "not ladylike" might communicate to the girl that she is not lovable when performing what otherwise seems to be exciting and fun. She is thus confronted with a threat to her self-concept (I am lovable) when she is behaving in a self-enhancing manner.

Since the threat to her self-concept must be removed, she may resolve the inconsistency in the phenomenal field by actualizing one behavior at one time and the other at another time. That is, she may be "ladylike" at home but climb trees when her parents are not around. She is thus maintaining all of her needs and she is experiencing both parts of her phenomenal field directly. However, if this possible solution is experienced as conflicting with a previously introjected value that, for instance, "deception is bad," she might have no recourse except to distort her own direct experience. Climbing trees may soon become in itself unpleasurable. It thus becomes lost to awareness within the phenomenal field. Potentiality for self-enhancement thus becomes more limited.

Defining our sex roles is just one example of an area in which we often introject values. That is, we define parts of our phenomenal field as meaningful on the basis of indirect experience. In a sense, however, all experience is direct. In the case of introjected values, what has been experienced directly is not the genuine immediate concern of the organism seeking self-enhancement, but rather the abiding relationship with others who have been evaluated as more important to the self-structure. It is because of this importance that the values so introjected became perceived in the phenomenal field as having been experienced directly.

There are, of course, a number of other examples that might have been used. Consider these rather common evaluations which are seldom experienced directly: (1) denial that some Catholics might be good by a person raised in a Baptist home, (2) belief that religious persons are necessarily irrational by a person raised by highly academic or atheistic parents, (3) belief that Mexicans in the southwest are dumb because they do not always speak proper English, (4) labeling of policemen as "fascist pigs" by a young freshman, newly introduced into collegiate society. All of these might lead to difficulty or strain, if any of the persons having introjected such values ever became open to a process of reevaluation. The concept of "openness" will be examined later.

11. As experiences occur in the life of the individual, they are either (a) symbolized, perceived, and organized into some relationship to the self, (b) ignored because there is no perceived relationship to the self-structure, or (c) denied symbolization or given a distorted symbolization because the experience is inconsistent with the structure of the self.

The term "awareness" has been used thus far to designate a certain portion of the phenomenal field. It should here be emphasized that the phenomenal field is not identical with the field of awareness or consciousness. According to Rogers, "consciousness is the symbolization of some of our experience." Thus, the phenomenal field is always made up of both conscious or *symbolized* experiences and unconscious or *unsymbolized* experiences. Primarily, we have been concerned with that behavior of the organism which reflects reactions to the symbolized field of experience. But the individual may, however, react as well to an experience which is not symbolized. Rogers calls this process *subception*.

Experiences which become symbolized are those that are perceived as enhancing the self-structure. If a hunter's self-structure includes a competitive need, that is, if self-enhancement is derived through being the best, coming home empty-handed from an outing might be perceived as an admission of failure. The day, thereby, may be perceived as having been a depressing waste of time. To his less competitive companion, however, the day may have been experienced as relaxing and enjoyable. The fact that no game was bagged is ignored, since this experience is perceived as having no relationship to the self-structure.

Denial or distortion in the symbolizing process may occur if the experience is perceived as being inconsistent with the self-structure. The unsuccessful hunter may distort his experience by saying, "This gun is too old," or "Everyone was too noisy." Responses which consistently distort experiences are commonly known as "rationalizations."

Perhaps these distortions are unimportant and actually cause little difficulty in our lives. Refusal to actualize basic organic experiences may, however, cause severe coping problems. When introjected values are prohibitive in relation to sexual strivings, natural organic experiences may be totally denied. "Sexual frigidity" would perhaps constitute such a case. The individual subceives such experiences which are threatening to the self-structure. Symbolization of a number of other experiences may occur instead in order to block out symbolization of the "true" experience. Anxiety and tension result from a number of such subceived experiences.

12. *Most of the ways of behaving which are adopted by the organism are those which are consistent with the concept of self.*

This principle is predictive of behavior that is in keeping with self-structure, even when the environment is providing stimuli to the contrary. The potentiality for a new experience may never make it into consciousness. A Protestant who enjoys traveling to the annual conventions of his particular denomination might not appreciate travel to Rome and the Vatican. A young adolescent male who desires to be a "real man" may well react negatively, if introduced to the possibilities for self-enhancement provided by a study of art, ballet, or even music. Consciously considering engaging in such activities, that is, allowing them a symbolized relationship to the self-structure, will probably never occur. If they should be so allowed, obviously a change in self-structure must occur.

13. *Behavior may, in some instances, be brought about by organic experiences and needs which have not been symbolized. Such behavior may be inconsistent with the structure of the self, but in such instances the behavior is not "owned" by the individual.*

Unsymbolized experience is reacted to as well as that which is symbolized. But the resulting behavior may appear as strange or unusual to the individual as it is to his friends. "He just really wasn't himself," may be their response. This happens, often, under the influence of alcohol or drugs or unusual pressure. It is possible that the self-structure becomes diffused, allowing non-symbolized experiences to be actualized. A person who becomes unusually angry may strike even those whom he, apparently, otherwise loves.

14. *Psychological maladjustment exists when the organism denies to awareness significant sensory and visceral experiences, which consequently are not symbolized and organized into the Gestalt of the self-structure. When this situation exists, there is a basic or potential psychological tension.*

This principle is perhaps a bit redundant. But the emphasis here on tension or possible maladjustment is quite significant. Even if experiences not allowed symbolization are not crucial to the organism, at the very least a loss of possible means for self-enhancement still ensues. If a number of experiences are perceived in a non-symbolized form, life might become very dull for the individual. This in itself might result in a continual state of tension for the organism. And, of course, as we saw with basic sexual strivings, an individual might suffer such maladjustments as to become unable even to react to the stimulation provided by a loved one.

15. *Psychological adjustment exists when the concept of the self is such that all the sensory and visceral experiences of the organism are, or may be, assimilated on a symbolic level into a consistent relationship with the concept of self.*

To illustrate this principle we need only refer to some of our previous examples. We examined the possibility of a young girl solving her dilemma by being "ladylike" at home and climbing trees when her parents are not around. She could, thereby, "realistically" symbolize both experiences and perhaps conceptualize herself as a young "lady" who likes to climb trees. Our empty-handed hunter might reappraise the condition of his gun, and finding no problem there, look elsewhere—perhaps to some need for practice on his own part.

A distinction should here be pointed out in regard to assimilation of experience into a relationship with the self-structure and the process of acting out that experience for the purpose of self-enhancement. Acting out or behaving in a fashion reflective of those experiences which are available to consciousness is not necessary in order to keep tension in abeyance. It is only necessary that such experience be symbolized. For instance, the young girl need not actually go and climb trees in order to reduce her internal conflict. It is only necessary for her to view this desire as consistent with a positive evaluation of her self-structure. She may choose to forego the pleasure, not because of possible negative evaluation by her parents, but simply because it might make her parents happier with themselves.

16. Any experience which is inconsistent with the organization or structure of self may be perceived as a threat, and the more of these perceptions there are the more rigidly the self-structure is organized to maintain itself.

If an individual has organized into his symbolized field a large number of introjected values, he may perceive experiences inconsistent with such values as threatening. In phenomenological terms his very being in the world is thereby denied expression. To avoid such a state of nonbeing, all being that is available to him must be so organized as to maintain that center—the self-structure—within the phenomenal field. Behavior is still characterized as purposive. But the purpose is narrowly defined. Consciousness undergoes contraction. Behavior may be observed as rigid, unpleasant, even in extreme cases as paranoid.

This principle, then, describes a circular process. The circle becomes, however, increasingly constricted and harder and harder to break out of. Consider this thought sequence by R. D. Liang:

> I want it
> I get it
> therefore I am good

I want it
I don't get it
therefore I am bad

I am bad because I didn't get it

I am bad because I wanted what I didn't get

I must take care
   to get what I want
   and want what I get
   and not get what I don't want[3]

To illustrate further, consider the stereotype provided by the poorer whites of the Southern states. Life is hard. The range of potential experiences for self-enhancement is narrow. In order to withstand such conditions it becomes seemingly advantageous to symbolize, that is, rationalize some explanation. "Suffering is God's will" may become such a rationalization. Or, "we white folks (meaning rich and poor as equals) are superior to darkies." Erich Fromm has suggested a similar process as having been characteristic of the German lower middle classes during the depression of the early 1930s. The Jews became their "scapegoat." German "greatness" was incorporated into their self-structure. In both cases experiences that might lead to a more "realistic" appraisal of their condition are perceived as threatening to a self which has incorporated racial prejudice into its structure. This narrowing of their experience thus provides a means by which they might at least temporarily endure the harsh conditions.

17. *Under certain conditions, involving primarily complete absence of any threat to the self-structure, experiences which are inconsistent with it may be perceived, and examined, and the structure of self revised to assimilate and include such experiences.*

This is, perhaps, the central premise underlying the entire approach to "client-centered therapy." It is Rogers' formula for breaking out of those circles, diagramed by Liang in his book *Knots*. Contained also in this principle is the key to Rogers' own particular contribution to psychology as a human science: existential phenomenology and empiricism are herein brought together and made compatible. And finally, a basis is here provided from which can be suggested a number of specific ways teachers, counselors, administrators, as well as therapists and simply good friends might build *helping relationships* with those in need that come their way.

The basic idea herein expressed is quite simple and common to our experience; it operates in all of our lives for those seemingly important, but often superficial distortions of our experience. For instance, we are more like our "true selves" around friends. That is, in the presence of an accepting person, we feel non-threatened and free to incorporate more of our experience into our self-structure. How often have you reflected upon something someone has said to you, something which had been earlier rejected as being "false" because it appeared threatening in the presence of that person, but which later seemed quite plausible? Your behavior, thus, underwent modification. You experienced an expansion of consciousness by allowing more of your experience to become symbolized. That is, your self-structure became reoriented toward the greater range of your entire phenomenal field.

In this principle Rogers has seemingly resolved the great paradox of phenomenology: how can one differentiate between a subjective image which is not a correct representation of reality from one that is. This is not to say that Rogers has specifically or intentionally entered the age-old philosophical debate on the issue of what constitutes reality. He has merely observed a process which seems to occur with his patients, or clients, as he prefers to call them. As a result, Rogers has actually redefined the phenomenological orientation somewhat. Instead of defining as "reality" that which is given in the experience of a person, he views such experience as constituting merely a tentative hypothesis about reality. This hypothesis may or may not be true. In fact, in any absolute respect, truth or falsity may itself be considered as irrelevant to the experience of the organism. What is relevant is the continual process which ensues as hypotheses are formed and tested, reformed and retested. Testing consists of checking the correctness, or *congruence*, of what is given in an experience with that given in other or additional experiences. Phenomenon experienced indirectly might be checked against that experienced more directly. Non-symbolized experience becomes increasingly symbolized and is organized into relationship with that which is already symbolized. Rogers considers the organism to be at all times a totally organized system in which alteration of any part may produce changes in any other part. But he also in this respect delineates four specific attitudes or modes of being, which, if incorporated into the self-structure, will facilitate this process of reality testing. These are: (1) openness to experience, (2) trust in the wisdom of the organism to maintain and enhance itself, (3) willingness to be a process, and (4) while in process—willingness to experience ambiguity.

This process of reality testing is then a process of experimenting with the possible range of experience available to the organism. When threat to the self is absent, experience can be perceived in differentiated fashion, that is, learning of new modes of being can proceed. But in the case of a more rigidly organized self-structure, the process may need facilitation by others. Rogers has elaborated upon those conditions necessary for an encounter between two people which will provide such facilitation. In 1958, in an address before the American Personnel and Guidance Association meeting in St. Louis, Rogers enumerated in the form of questions "The Characteristics of a Helping Relationship":

1. Can I *be* in some way which will be perceived by the other person as trustworthy . . . dependably real? By this I mean that whatever feeling or attitude I am experiencing would be matched by my awareness of that attitude . . . and hence I can *be* whatever I deeply *am*.

2. Can I be expressive enough as a person that what I am will be communicated unambiguously? If I can be sensitively aware of and acceptant toward my own feelings, then the likelihood is great that I can form a helping relationship toward another.

3. Can I let myself experience positive attitudes toward this other person —attitudes of warmth, caring, liking, interest, respect? . . .

4. Can I be strong enough as a person to be separate from others? . . . I find that I can let myself go much more deeply in understanding and accepting, because I am not fearful of losing myself.

5. Am I secure enough within myself to permit him his separateness? Can I permit him to be what he is—honest or deceitful, infantile or adult, despairing or over-confident? Or do I feel that he should follow my advice, mold himself after me?

6. Can I let myself enter fully into the world of his feelings and personal meanings? Can I step into his private world so completely that I lose all desire to evaluate or judge it?

7. Can I be acceptant of each facet of this other person? Can I revere him as he is? Or can I only accept him conditionally? It has been my experience that when my attitude is conditional, then he cannot change or grow in those respects in which I cannot fully receive him.

8. Can I act with sufficient sensitivity in the relationship that my behavior will not be perceived as a threat? . . . if I can free him as completely as possible from external threat, then he can begin to experience and to deal with the internal feelings and conflicts which he finds threatening within himself.

9. Can I free him from the threat of external evaluation? . . . the more I can keep a relationship free of judgment and evaluation (good or bad), the more this will permit the other person to recognize that the center of responsibility lies within himself.

10. Can I meet this other individual as a person who is in the process of becoming, or will I be bound by his past and by my past? If I accept the other person as diagnosed and classified, then I am doing my part to confirm this limited hypothesis. If I accept him as a process of becoming, then I am doing what I can to confirm or make real his potentialities.[4]

This particular principle along with Rogers' elaboration on the necessary and sufficient conditions for positive growth — those characteristics of a helping relationship — provide the basis of what amounts to an empirical theory of behavior modification from a phenomenological standpoint, to borrow the term from behavior psychology. Rogers himself has suggested that the scientific method itself might provide a basis for rapprochement between "these two divergent currents, whose advocates often find communication difficult because their differences are so great."[5] He thus defended his approach to therapy as reflecting a genuinely scientific orientation:

They say, "Some efforts to be therapeutic, to bring about constructive change, are effective; others are not. We find that there are certain characteristics that differentiate the two classes. We find, for example, that in the helpful relationships, it is likely that the therapist functions as a real person, interacting with his real feelings. In the less helpful relationships, we frequently find that the therapist functions as an intelligent manipulator, rather than as his real self." Here too is a perfectly legitimate concept of science, the detecting of the order which is inherent in any given series of events. I submit that this second conception is more likely to discover the uniquely human aspects of therapy.[6]

In addition to having reported, in the address on characteristics of a helping relationships, on the extensive research already completed and then underway, Rogers later in cooperation with Rollo May suggested these "testable hypotheses" as examples of how "our positivist tradition of operational definitions and empirical research might be helpful in investigating the truth of ontological principles":

1. The more the self of the person is threatened, the more he will exhibit defensive neurotic behavior . . . and the more his ways of being and behavior will become constricted.
2. The more the self is free from threat, the more the individual will exhibit self-affirming behavior . . . and the more he will exhibit the need for, and the actualization of, participant behavior.
3. A specific anxiety will be resolved only if the client loses the fear of being the specific potentiality regarding which he has been anxious.[7]

Rogers thus anticipates that the involvement of psychological science in these "subtle, subjective, and value permeated fields" will hopefully induce the next step in the evolution of the scientific method.[8]

18. *When the individual perceives and accepts into one consistent and integrated system all his sensory and visceral experiences, then he is necessarily more understanding of others and is more accepting of others as separate individuals.*

19. *As the individual perceives and accepts into his self-structure more of his organic experience, he finds that he is replacing his present value system — based so largely upon introjections which have been distortedly symbolized — with a continuing organismic valuing process.*

In these two principles, Rogers pulls together the various threads regarding the phenomenological behavior of the human organism into one descriptive strand — what amounts to, in traditional therapeutic schools, as a definition of positive mental health. This definition was later elaborated by Rogers and given a much more phenomenological title: "The Concept of the Fully Functioning Person." This concept provides then, for Rogers a hypothetical end-point, the ultimate, of the therapeutic process.

A fully functioning person, an ideal type of course, lives fully on and with each and all of his feelings and reactions. He is able to be at each moment what he potentially is. That is, he is open to and trusts in his total organismic being. He permits his organism to function within the total range of his phenomenal field, selecting from the multitude of possible experiences to actualize in behavior those which in this moment of time will be most generally and genuinely satisfying. He exists as a process of being and becoming himself.

Since such a person is open to his world of experience and trusts in his own ability to interact directly with that world, always thereby forming new relationships within his phenomenal field, his life style would certainly be characterized as creative. And although he would not necessarily be adjusted to his culture, that is, he would not be simply a conformist (introjected values), he would be able at any time and in any culture to live both creatively and in as much harmony with that culture as a balanced satisfaction of needs demanded.

From the point of view of an observer of such a person's behavior, he would appear as constructive and trustworthy. Concern for his "proper socialization" need not exist — the need of unusually oppressive social systems notwithstanding, such as exists under totalitarian regimes—since one of his own deepest needs is affiliation and communication with others. Aggressive impulses will, within the context of his being open to all of his experience, be balanced and synthesized in his own creative manner with his tendency to give and receive affection from others. His total behavior will be balanced, realistic and appropriate to maintain and enhance his organism.

One final characteristic of such an ideally functioning person has particular implications for a humanistically based approach to psychology. Rogers has found disturbing the commonly held prerequisite that psychology as a science concern itself with the prediction and control of human behavior. He offers a distinction between discovering in a post-dict fashion behavior to be lawful and prediction of behavior by previously formulated laws. In fact, it is only the maladjusted individual whose behavior can be, to some degree, specifically predicted. This is so precisely because such an individual's reaction to his phenomenal field will be rigidly patterned. The behavior of a fully functioning person is, on the other hand, not predictable in advance, although nevertheless lawful in the sense of being dependable. This is to say, that his behavior may be depended upon in that he will always react in an enhancing manner to all the complex evidence which is immediately given in his phenomenal field of experience. Rogers points out that only a "computer of great size" could specifically predict the behavior of such an individual, and even then it would be necessarily post-dictive—since, existentially speaking, a person fully open to his experience, completely without defensiveness, creates himself anew at each moment, in every action taken, in every decision made.

humanistic

CHAPTER 8

Implications for Teaching:
The Facilitation of Learning

In this chapter we will consider the implications of Carl Rogers' view of human nature and existence specifically for education. In a number of articles and books Rogers has advocated what amounts to a revolution in education. He hesitates, however, to use that term for fear "that this might offend and antagonize too many people." But he nevertheless believes that "only a tremendous change in the basic direction of education can meet the needs of today's culture."[1] The goal for our educational system, from nursery school through graduate school, must derive from the dynamic nature of our society, a society characterized by change not tradition, by process not static rigidity. Within this system, must be developed a climate conducive to personal growth, a climate in which innovation is not at all frightening, in which creative capacities of all concerned are nourished and expressed rather than stifled. Only in this way can the individual working within our system—whether he be student, teacher, or administrator—be provided the opportunity for maximum experiential striving in his personal quest for enhancement. The end-point of our educational system, according to Rogers, no less than that of theory, must be the development of "fully functioning" people.

In an address to educators at Harvard University, an address which he himself reports to have been received with furious criticism, Rogers made such confessions as: (1) "My experience has been that I cannot teach another person to teach," (2) furthermore, "I have come to feel that the outcomes of teaching are either unimportant or hurtful," (3) "I realize that I have lost interest in being a teacher," and (4) "I realize that I am only interested in being a learner."[2]

These statements may seem surprising and even offensive to the reader. But they are consistent with a phenomenological view of man. For instance, as soon as focus is given to the activity of teaching, the

116

question arises, what shall be taught? What, from the "superior" vantage point of the teacher, does the student need to know? Can a teacher really be sure of his answer to such a question? Or, what shall the course cover? Any answer given to this question presupposes that what is taught is what is learned; what is presented is what is assimilated. Furthermore, this assumption is usually followed by another: what is assimilated can be accurately measured by some means, such as examination. But all such assumptions run counter to that view of man which postulates individual freedom and uniqueness. And they all become either harmful or useless in the face of the above view which postulates the inherent strivings of the organism for maintenance and enhancement. The implication is, of course, that our present system lacks trust in the human organism; it denies man both his freedom and his dignity.

Rogers postulates that the goal of education, if we are to survive, must become the facilitation of change and learning. By this view, the only man who is educated is the man who has learned how to learn; the man who has learned how to adapt and change, who realizes that no knowledge is secure and that only the process of seeking knowledge gives any basis for security. Only from an interpersonal context in which learning is facilitated will arise "true students, real learners, creative scientists and scholars, and practitioners, the kind of individuals who can live in a delicate but ever changing balance between what is presently known and the flowing, moving, changing problems and facts of the future."[3]

The facilitation of learning is not equivalent to teaching as commonly defined. It does not necessarily, for instance, rely upon any particular skills of the leader, nor upon his scholarly knowledge, nor upon his curricular planning, nor upon the use of audiovisual aids. It does not depend upon programed learning, lectures, oral reports or even books and pencils and paper. Any of these, of course, might be utilized as a resource. In fact, a facilitator of learning is primarily just that in relationship to the learner, a resource. But as a living resource the facilitator can only function in an interpersonal relationship with the learner. It is this relationship which must, therefore, be of prime importance in any educational setting.

Rogers has discerned certain atitudinal qualities which exist in the interpersonal relationship between facilitator and learner. It is upon these that the facilitation of significant learning finally rests. Note the close similarity of these qualities to those also seen by Rogers to be necessary in any successful therapeutic encounter.

The first of these essential attitudes is realness or genuineness. A teacher to be a facilitator must discard the traditional "role," "mask," "facade" of being "The Teacher" and become a real person with his students. This means that whatever feelings he is having he can accept in himself and not hide from his students. If he is bored or angry or enthusiastic or sympathetic, he can be so freely without having to impose these on his students. Students are left free to respond in like manner. For instance, the teacher may express like or dislike for a student product without implying that it is objectively good or bad or that the student is good or bad.

A good example of this attitude of realness and the prerequisite of self-knowledge that it requires is furnished by a sixth-grade teacher, whose experiment in creating a self-directed classroom setting was reported on at length by Rogers in his book *Freedom to Learn*. Being continually upset and distracted by a continually messed-up room, the teacher announced that *she* had a problem. Namely, that she found it difficult to work in all the mess. She asked the group if they could help her, and they responded by setting up a cleaning system. This teacher was genuine in that she recognized that her need for cleanliness was her need, not necessarily anyone else's. She was not judgmental. The students were not reprimanded for being bad. Uncleanliness was not equated with any moral absolute. The students responded out of respect for a minority need. They too were genuine, and they were both free and responsible.

A second attitude which must pervade the facilitator-learner relationship is that born of an abiding trust and acceptance, even a prizing of the other person as a worthy, valuable individual. It involves caring, but not of a possessive or controlling nature. It is acceptance of the other as a separate person, as having worth in his own right, and as being entitled to the full opportunity of seeking out, experimenting, and discovering that which is enhancing to self. Since learning may often involve a change in the organization of the self, it occurs more frequently when external threats to the self are at a minimum. A teacher experiencing this attitude of trust can accept in a non-judgmental fashion student apathy, erratic desires, perhaps even rejection of the teacher's suggestions, as well as disciplined effort to achieve chosen goals. In trusting the student, the teacher is actually, thereby, expressing his own essential confidence and trust in the capacity of his own organismic being.

And finally, in any relationship where learning is to occur, communication must ensue between those persons involved. And communication is by nature only possible in a climate characterized by empathic understanding. A facilitator of learning must be sensitively aware of the way the process of education and learning seems to the student. Rogers maintains that this kind of non-evaluative understanding is practically unheard of in the average classroom. Learners, if they are to succeed at their chosen tasks, need communication. They need to be understood, not evaluated, not judged, not taught. Facilitation requires acceptant, empathic understanding.

Rogers has cited several examples of empirical research that have tended to verify in more traditional terms of educational success the approach exemplified in these three attitudes. Six third-grade teachers tape-recorded two full weeks of interaction with their students in the period devoted to the teaching of reading. In order to obtain an adequate sampling of these interactions the recordings were made two months apart. Segments of four minutes each were selected at random for rating by persons working independently and "blind." Being rated were the three attitudinal qualities: degree of genuineness shown by the teacher, degree of unconditional positive regard, and the degree of empathic understanding.

The criteria used were traditional (Stanford) achievement tests. As predicted, gains in reading achievement were greater in those classes which had been characterized by a proportionately higher degree of these attitudes. Rogers concludes with a certain degree of assurance, therefore, that these attitudes which he has endeavored to qualitatively delineate are, in fact, ". . . not only effective in facilitating a deeper learning and understanding of self in a relationship such as psychotherapy, but that these attitudes characterize teachers who are regarded as effective teachers, and that the students of these teachers learn more, even of a conventional curriculum, than do students of teachers who are lacking in these attitudes."[4]

The achievement of these attitudes is no easy task. Yet we experience them any time we really communicate with others. Basic to all of these attitudes is trust in the capacity of the human individual for developing his own potentiality. Only with this trust can learning be facilitated, opportunities provided, freedom given. A facilitator works on the hypothesis that any student who is in real contact with problems deemed relevant to himself will want to learn, to grow, to discover, to create, to become self-disciplined. Only slowly, perhaps, can these attitudes be truly realized in a classroom situation. But only if they are realized can learning become, in that oftentimes falsified atmosphere, what learning truly is, the very vital striving of the organism for life itself.

Thus, the kind of learning being facilitated within this interpersonal relationship will be self-initiated. Rogers considers learning to have been facilitated when the student participates responsibly in the learning process. Self-initiated learning involves the whole person of the learner (feelings as well as intellect) and is the most lasting and pervasive. Furthermore, learning to be a learner, that is, to be independent, creative, and self-reliant is better facilitated when self-criticism and self-evaluation are basic and evaluation by others is of secondary importance. This is, of course, learning the process of learning. It is being continually open to experience and incorporation into oneself of the very process of change.

The classroom atmosphere then must be student-centered. The facilitator must try to draw out from the student those problems or issues which are real for him. Ideally, this would not, of course, be necessary. But the fact is that since in general students are so insulated from problems, it may be necessary to confront them with situations which will become real problems to them. Oftentimes, however, this may also simply be a matter of allowing natural confrontations to occur. How many of our schools really desire to teach democratic values? What better way to teach about political processes in a high school, for instance, then by allowing students maximum self-government? If students were free from so many of those rules imposed from above and without, they would, from the necessity of their own social interaction, formulate laws designed to enhance those reasons for their coming together.

This idea was, of course, the central premise of Locke's democratic political philosophy. And in this sense, Rogers is actually very much in the Lockean tradition. If student self-government seems too "far out," the reader is referred to A. S. Neil's *Summerhill*. Summerhill is a self-governing school. Everything connected with the social interaction of its members, including even punishment for social offenses, is settled by vote at Saturday night general school meetings. Each child, regardless of age, has one vote. And so does each staff member, including Neil himself. Consider Rogers' own strong opinion regarding this "radical approach to child rearing":

It raises profound questions about most of our ways of dealing with children. It pictures an exciting alternative to those procedures. It also gives us a most encouraging realization that when children are given a responsible freedom, in a climate of understanding and non-possessive love, they choose with wisdom, learn with alacrity, and develop genuinely social attitudes. I find that this corresponds with what I have learned in psychotherapy. I commend this book to every open-minded person who is concerned with the reduction of hate and aggression and fear in the world, and who is eager for children and adults to live full lives.[5]

But even within our schools as they are now organized there is much opportunity for reform in a humanistic direction. For instance, a teacher endeavoring to facilitate truly experiential learning may himself learn to avoid organizing his time around preparing lectures, lesson plans, and examinations; rather, he might concentrate on making resources clearly available. He thinks through and simplifies the practical and psychological steps which the individual student must go through in order to utilize a particular source. As a human resource he is himself introductory material to a wider world of potential experience to the learner. Unfortunately, state certification requirements often tend to disqualify persons with a truly wide range of life and work experience. This is due, of course, to their functional design, the recruitment of teachers as opposed to facilitators of learning. Rogers observes that by the time the child has spent a number of years in school, intrinsic motivation may well be dampened. Yet it is always there, waiting to be tapped.

A number of contemporary reforms in school curriculum actually do reflect a growing demand for a somewhat humanistic educational approach. Jerome Bruner in *The Process of Education* has called for such changes as would redesign the study of every traditional subject. The new design would center on the activity of "inquiry" or discovery learning. This is, of course, learning by doing. Students become self-directed researchers, scientists themselves, on a simple level. They seek answers to real questions, experiencing in themselves the pains and joys of inquiry. They may not learn as many "facts," but they learn the process by which facts become and unbecome, are accepted as such and later rejected. They learn how to learn.

Similar to "inquiry learning" is the experiential learning entailed in "simulation." Real-life situations are simulated with as much of their complexity and urgency as possible. To play-act at governing a nation may not be quite as "real" as governing your own life, but given the typical school organization, it does have its merits. Students develop disciplined commitment and experience a sense of personal involvement in, and responsibility for, decisions made and action taken.

Rogers does not hesitate also to recommend both his own favorite medium for genuine and meaningful learning, the basic encounter group, as well as that tool provided by the behaviorists, programed instruction. With the latter is provided an excellent means by which a student may fill in the gaps in the information he needs to meet whatever problem he is confronting. In this sense, the very flexibility of programed instruction lends itself to individualized facilitation in a classroom setting. However, it should never become a substitute for thinking in larger patterns. If it becomes a way of emphasizing factual knowledge as compared to the creative processes entailed in genuine inquiry and discovery, then damage may well be done to the learner.

Since the early 1960s Rogers has written and spoken extensively on what has become one of the most widespread and practical contributions of humanistic psychology, the encounter group (known also as the "T" group, laboratory training, sensitivity training, and workshop). Regardless of the name used, the general aim of these intensive group experiences has been to improve and facilitate self-learning and interpersonal communication. In fact, it has also been referred to as a journey to the center of the self. Rogers views the encounter group as a tool with tremendous potential for educational change. And actually, many have hailed it as having an even wider potential, that is, as constituting a genuine solution to the problem of alienation in our increasingly complex and materialistic society.

An encounter group usually consists of 10 to 15 people, along with a facilitator or group leader. The group is relatively unstructured and characterized by a climate of freedom for the expression of personal feelings and interpersonal communication. The word "encounter" refers to that interaction which occurs when people drop their defenses and facades and relate directly and openly as "real" persons. The atmosphere thus created is like that found in client-centered therapy. The trust that is generated enables a person to recognize, experiment, and exchange self-defeating attitudes for those more conducive to innovative and constructive behavior. Followup studies indicate that the person is able to relate more adequately and effectively to others in his everyday situation.

Rogers suggests that in the educational setting the encounter group may be used to release the capacity of participants for better educational leadership through improved interpersonal relationships and to facilitate learning by the whole person. In his book *Freedom to Learn*, the last chapter provides a plan, within the context of specific suggestions, for implementing changes in any given school system during a relatively short period of time. The emphasis is on the whole system, including administrators, teachers, students, and parents. He suggests that persons meet in these separate groups and later in a vertical group which would be constituted by a cross-section of the entire educational system.

Changes and innovations which are decided upon during an intensive group experience are actually more likely to be implemented than otherwise. People are less resistant to change when they do not feel threatened and when they are determining these changes themselves. The exercise of freedom is inseparable from the burden of responsibility. And that burden may actually become lighter and even fulfilling in a climate of trust and positive regard.

Rogers maintains, then, that the effect of encounter groups on teachers and students may be reasonably well predicted. Teachers will be more able really to listen to students, especially to their feelings. They will be more likely to work out interpersonal difficulties with students, rather than become punitive and disciplinarian. The classroom atmosphere will become more equalitarian, conducive to spontaneity and creative thinking, and to independent, self-directed work. Students will discover their own individual responsibility for their own learning. They will have more energy to devote to learning and will feel free to pursue self-chosen avenues of learning. Learning, in fact, will become a much more intensive and personally relevant activity. A student's awe of authority and his rebellion against authority will diminish as discovery is made that teachers and administrators are, after all, also human—fallible, imperfect, but also striving for meaning and enhancement.

Notes

PREFACE

1. Ernest R. Hilgard, *Theories of Learning* (New York: Appleton-Century-Crofts, Inc., 1st ed. 1948, 2nd ed. 1965, 3rd ed. with Gordon H. Bower, 1966).
2. Gordon Allport, *Becoming* (New Haven: Yale University Press, 1955).
3. T. W. Wann (ed.), *Behaviorism and Phenomenology: Contrasting Bases for Modern Psychology* (Chicago: University of Chicago Press, 1964).
4. William D. Hitt, "Two Models of Man," *American Psychologist,* Vol. XXIV, No. 7 (July, 1969).

CHAPTER 1

1. K. Jaspers, *Philosophy Is for Everyman* (New York: Harcourt, Brace & World, 1967), pp. 242-43.
2. Rollo May (ed.), *Existential Psychology*, A. H. Maslow, "Existential Psychology—What's in It for Us?" (New York: Random House, 1961), p. 59.

CHAPTER 2

1. Gordon Allport, *Becoming* (New Haven: Yale University Press, 1955), pp. 8-12.
2. Ibid., p. 7.
3. Ibid., p. 8.
4. Edna Heidbreder, *Seven Psychologies* (New York: D. Appleton-Century Co., 1933).

PART II

1. B. F. Skinner, *Walden Two* (New York: Macmillan, 1948).
2. B. F. Skinner, *Beyond Freedom and Dignity* (New York: Alfred A. Knopf, 1971).

CHAPTER 3

1. B. F. Skinner, *Behavior of Organisms: An Experimental Analysis* (New York: Appleton-Century-Crofts, 1938).
2. B. F. Skinner, *Science and Human Behavior* (New York: Macmillan, 1953), p. 23.
3. Carl R. Rogers and B. F. Skinner, "Some Issues Concerning the Control of Human Behavior," *Science*, Vol. CXXIV, No. 3231 (November 30, 1956).

CHAPTER 4

1. B. F. Skinner, *Science and Human Behavior* (New York: Macmillan, 1953), pp. 85-87.

2. Ibid., p. 132.

3. Ibid., p. 94.

4. Ibid., pp. 63 ff.

5. Ellen Reese, *The Analysis of Human Operant Behavior* (Dubuque, Iowa: William C. Brown, 1966), p. 14.

6. B. F. Skinner, op. cit., p. 91.

7. Ibid., p. 183.

8. Fred S. Keller, *Learning: Reinforcement Theory* (New York: Random House, 1954), p. 24.

9. A. Bandura and Richard H. Walters, *Social Learning and Personality Development* (New York: Holt, Rinehart and Winston, Inc., 1963).

CHAPTER 5

1. B. F. Skinner, *The Technology of Teaching* (New York: Appleton-Century-Crofts, 1968), p. 40.

2. Ibid., p. 45.

3. Ibid., p. 119.

4. Richard I. Evans, *B. F. Skinner: The Man and His Ideas* (New York: E. P. Dutton & Co., Inc., 1968), pp. 30-31.

CHAPTER 6

1. Quoted in Gardner Murphy, *Historical Introduction to Modern Psychology* (New York: Harcourt, Brace & World, 1949), p. 67.

2. Quoted in Rollo May, *Psychology and the Human Dilemma* (New York: D. Van Nostrand Company, Inc., 1967), p. 111.

3. Ibid., p. 25.

4. David Ausubel, *Theory and Problem of Child Development* (New York: Grune & Stratton, 1957), p. 43.

5. Maurice Friedman, *To Deny Our Nothingness: Contemporary Images of Man* (New York: Dell Publishing Co., Inc., 1967).

6. H. A. Hodges, *The Philosophy of Wilhelm Dilthey* (London: Routledge, 1952), pp. xiv-xv.

7. H. A. Hodges, *Wilhelm Dilthey: An Introduction* (London: Routledge, 1944), p. 42.

8. William R. Coulion and Carl R. Rogers (eds.), *Man and the Science of Man*, "Some Thoughts Regarding the Current Presuppositions of the Behavioral Sciences" (Columbus, Ohio: Charles E. Merrill Publishing Co.), p. 69.

9. William James, *The Principles of Psychology*, Vol. I (New York: Henry Holt & Co., 1890), p. 7.

10. Quoted in William R. Coulion and Carl R. Rogers (eds.), op. cit., p. vii.

11. Quoted in Rollo May, op. cit., p. 182.

12. Quoted in ibid., p. 139.

13. Maurice Friedman (ed.), *The Worlds of Existentialism: A Critical Reader* (New York: Random House, 1964), p. 3.

14. Maurice Friedman, *To Deny Our Nothingness: Contemporary Images of Man*, p. 254.

15. Quoted in ibid., pp. 246-47.

16. Rollo May (ed.), Gordon Allport, "Comment on Earlier Chapters," *Existential Psychology* (New York: Random House, 1961), pp. 44-45.

17. Ibid., Carl R. Rogers, "Two Divergent Trends," p. 87.

18. Rollo May, op. cit., p. 15.

CHAPTER 7

1. Carl R. Rogers, "A Theory of Therapy, Personality, and Inter-Personal Relationships, as Developed in the Client-Centered Framework," in S. Koch (ed.), *Psychology: A Study of Science*, Vol. III (New York: McGraw-Hill, 1959), pp. 200-01.

2. Ibid., p. 200.

3. R. D. Liang, *Knots* (New York: Random House, 1970), p. 38.

4. Carl R. Rogers, "The Characteristics of a Helping Relationship," *Personnel Guidance Journal*, 1958, Vol. XXXVII, pp. 6-16.

5. Carl R. Rogers, "Two Divergent Trends," in Rollo May (ed.), *Existential Psychology* (New York: Random House, 1961), p. 89.

6. Ibid.

7. Ibid., p. 90.

8. Ibid.

CHAPTER 8

1. Carl R. Rogers, *Freedom to Learn* (Columbus, Ohio: Charles E. Merrill Publishing Co.), p. 303.

2. Ibid., p. 151.

3. Ibid., p. 105.

4. Ibid., p. 119.

5. Quoted by publisher in A. S. Neil, *Summerhill: A Radical Approach to Child Rearing* (New York: Hart Publishing Co., 1960).

Bibliography

BRUNER, JEROME S. *The Process of Education.* New York: Random House, 1963. This book is the report of a conference of scientists and teachers, called together to discuss the improvement of science teaching in the schools. It is, in fact, a searching discussion of school education which proposes the adoption of the "inquiry method" as a basis for learning and teaching. Such a method is suggested by Rogers to be by nature facilitative.

HILL, WINFRED F. *Learning: A Survey of Psychological Interpretations,* rev. ed. Scranton, 1971. For anyone interested in a survey of learning theories, this is a very readable and solid presentation. Some effort is made to provide illustrations in an educational context, although the orientation is largely psychological.

LaBENNE, WALLACE D., and GREEN, BERT I. *Educational Implications of Self-Concept Theory.* Pacific Palisades, California: Goodyear Publishing Co., Inc., 1969. Provides empirical and experimental data demonstrating a direct phenomenological relationship between the child and his manifest behavior in terms of academic performance. The probable consequences of teaching activities on the developing self-concept of the child are carefully considered. And current educational practices are evaluated in terms of whether they enhance or damage the self-structure of the student.

MAY, ROLLO. *Psychology and the Human Dilemma.* Princeton, New Jersey: D. Van Nostrand Co., Inc., 1966. This book constitutes an analysis of the relationship between existentialism and a phenomenologically based approach to psychology. It is recommended for the mature student who wishes to investigate existential psychology at a more in-depth level.

———— (ed.). *Existential Psychology.* New York: Random House, 1960. The articles herein contained were originally presented in a symposium at the Annual Convention of the American Psychological Association in Cincinnati in September, 1959. The rather personal reasons for the participants becoming interested in the relationship between existential philosophy and psychology constitute the main theme of the book. The book is an excellent introductory presentation of this relationship. Articles are by Rogers, Maslow, Allport, and Feifel.

PITTENGER, OWEN, E., and GOODING, C. THOMAS. *Learning Theories in Educational Practice: An Integration of Psychological Theory and Educational Philosophy*. New York: John Wiley & Sons, Inc., 1971. Specific and prominent theories of learning are described and their implied assumptions about the nature of man and the conditions that promote learning are made explicit. Information is derived from various experimental and theoretical statements about the nature of learning. These theories are presented in a contrasting manner in order to facilitate understanding.

ROGERS, CARL R. *Freedom to Learn*. Columbus, Ohio: Charles E. Merrill Publishing Co., 1969. Pervading this book is the phenomenological orientation of Rogers in psychology and particularly in client-centered therapy. The result is an advocation of student-centered education. Specific means are suggested by which teachers may risk themselves in experimentation with their classes. A conceptual basis is provided for such experimentation as well as a presentation of the personal and philosophical underpinnings and ramifications of the whole approach. And finally, a specific program for bringing about self-directed change in an entire educational system is also presented.

———— and SKINNER, B. F. "Some Issues Concerning the Control of Human Behavior," *Science*, Vol. CXXIV, No. 3231 (November 30, 1956). This article is the written account of a symposium with Skinner and Rogers. Both psychologists present and defend their respective orientations in the light of the particular social, scientific, and philosophical implications. It is an excellent introduction to the seeming conflict between the two scientists.

SKINNER, B. F. *The Technology of Teaching*. New York: Appleton-Century-Crofts, 1968. Composed of a few previously published articles, addresses which had not been published, and several chapters written especially for the book, this book explains Skinner's views of the teaching-learning process. Teaching machines and programed instruction are described and the technology of teaching elaborated upon. Chapters on thinking, motivation, creativity, discipline, and teaching are directed primarily to educators.

————. *Walden Two*. New York: Macmillan, 1948. A serious argument for a controlled utopian society, this novel has continued to stimulate controversy since its publication in 1948. Walden Two is an economically self-sufficient rural community run on Skinnerian principles. Children are conditioned by professionals to behave in a manner that will insure their own happiness, their freedom from intellectual and moral struggles, and the continued stability of the community.

WANN, T. W. (ed.). *Behaviorism and Phenomenology: Contrasting Bases for Modern Psychology*. Chicago: University of Chicago Press, 1964. The articles herein contained were originally presented at a symposium at Rice University. The historical and philosophical backgrounds as well as the contemporary status of these two approaches to psychology constitute the primary focus of the book. Both Skinner and Rogers were among the participants.